LINDA COLLISTER
FOOD PROCESSOR
COOKERY

LINDA COLLISTER
FOOD PROCESSOR
C O O K E R Y

CONTENTS

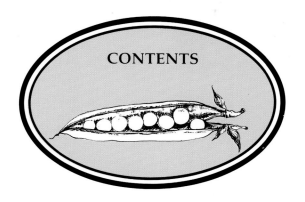

Introduction *6*

Soups and Appetizers *10*

Salads and Vegetables *30*

Meat and Poultry *49*

Fish and Shellfish *73*

Puddings and Desserts *94*

Cakes, Biscuits and Scones *114*

A QUINTET BOOK

Published by Apple Press Ltd
293 Gray's Inn Road
London WC1X 8QF

Copyright © 1984 Quintet
Publishing Limited
All rights reserved. No part of this
publication may be reproduced,
stored in a retrieval system, or
transmitted, in any form or by any
means, electronic, mechanical,
photocopying, recording or
otherwise, without the permission
of the copyright holder.

ISBN 1 85076 014 4

The Publishers wish to thank
Magimix for the use of their food
processor in the preparation of all
the dishes in this book.
The Publishers also wish to thank
Tower Housewares,
Wolverhampton and Pyrex,
London, for supplying the
kitchenware used in this book.

This book was designed and
produced by Quintet Publishing
Limited 32 Kingly Court,
London W1

Art Design Bridgewater Associates
Illustrator Lorraine Harrison
Photographer John Heseltine
Cookery Consultant Myra Street
Editor Cheen Horn

Typeset by Context Typesetting,
Brighton
Colour Origination in Hong Kong
by Hong Kong Graphic Arts
Limited
Printed in Hong Kong by Leefung-
Asco Printers Limited

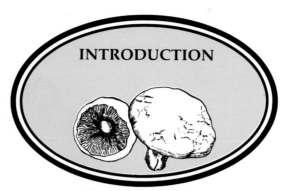

INTRODUCTION

Your processor is an investment, and it makes sense to look after it properly.

After each use, the base should be wiped with a damp cloth – it must never be immersed in water. Wash the bowls and blades in very hot water and dry well (or place in the dishwasher), then store with the pusher removed from the feed tube to avoid the bowl smelling musty.

The best way to store your blades and discs is in a special rack attached to a wall, out of reach of children. This will prevent accidents – the blades are very sharp, and also prevent the discs becoming dented and misshapen.

When using your processor the most important point to remember is not to overload or overwork your machine. Most machines have an automatic cut-out, which operates when the machine overheats or is labouring. It is quicker to prepare food in several batches, rather than overload the machine, then have to wait for it to cool down – maybe for 30 minutes. Don't try to process really hard foods, such as rock-hard parmesan cheese, coffee beans, bones, shells and gristle or you will damage or blunt your blades.

When pushing food down the feed tube, always use the plastic pusher provided – never use your fingers, or a knife or spoon or any other utensil.

Because most processors are very powerful and efficient it is only too easy to overprocess food at first, and coarsely chopped nuts suddenly become finely ground. So until you get the hang of your machine, use the pulse button, or keep stopping and starting the machine, when you need to chop or grind.

Overprocessing pastry and cakes will make them tough and heavy, so watch them carefully. If you leave the pusher out of the feed tube, it helps air to be incorporated into the dough.

I hope you will have fun using your processor. I have become addicted to mine, and can't imagine cooking without it now. It really is like having an extra pair of hands!

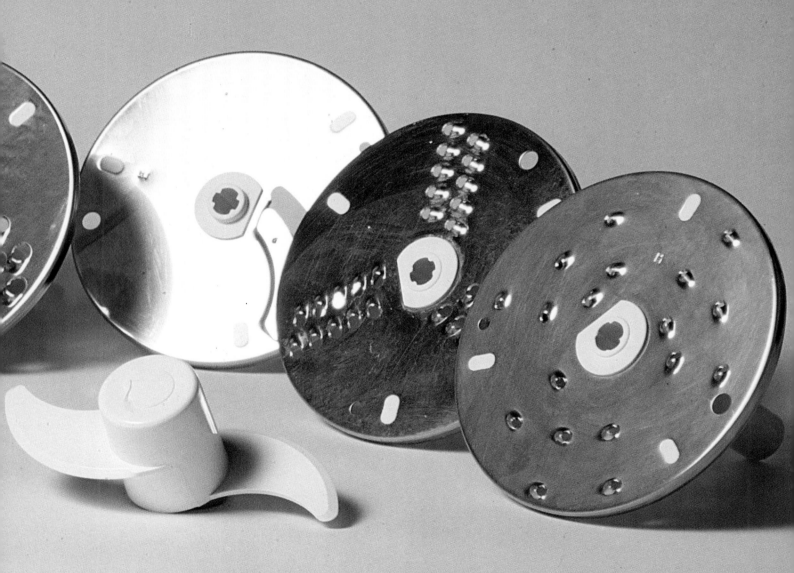

SOUPS AND APPETIZERS

Cheesy Potato Soup 12

Courgette (Zucchini) and Fennel Soup 13

Fresh Tomato and Vodka Soup 14

Country Vegetable Soup 15

Curried Lentil Soup 16

Quick Chilled Summer Soup 17

A Carrot Soup from Germany 18

Oriental Chicken Soup 19

Gazpacho 20

Cheesy Onion Quiche 22

Avocado and Blue Cheese Starter 23

Easy Liver Pâté 24

Kipper Mousse Quiche 25

Quick Blue Cheese Pâté 26

Asparagus and Egg Napoleon 27

Crunchy Pepper and Tuna Mousse 28

Herby Roulade 29

CHEESY POTATO SOUP

A substantial main course soup, only for the very hungry!

Serves 4 to 6
2 large / 450 g / 1 lb potatoes, peeled
2 large onions, peeled and quartered
2 cloves garlic, peeled
6 tbsp / 75 g / 3 oz butter or margarine
salt and freshly ground pepper
4¼ cups / 1 litre / 1¾ pints beef stock
1 cup / 100 g / 4 oz Cheddar cheese
Garnish: thin slices toasted French bread with a little extra grated cheese

Trim the potatoes to fit the feed tube. Using the slicing disc, slice the potatoes, onions and garlic. Heat the butter or margarine in a large, heavy pan and add the sliced vegetables with a little salt and pepper. Stir well, cover and simmer for about 10 minutes, or until the vegetables are softened and slightly golden in colour. Add the stock and simmer gently for 15 to 20 minutes, or until the soup has thickened and the vegetables are very tender.

Meanwhile, grate the cheese using the grating disc. Strain the soup, reserving the liquid. Using the metal blade process the vegetables until smooth, then return to the liquid with the grated cheese. Reheat, stirring constantly until the soup is thick and creamy. Taste for seasoning. To serve, toast bread and then cover with grated cheese, then grill (broil) until brown and bubbling. Spoon the soup into warmed bowls, and float cheese-topped toast slices on top.

COURGETTE (ZUCCHINI) AND FENNEL SOUP

This Italian soup is delicious served with garlic bread.

Serves 4 to 6
1 bulb fennel, approx. 225 g / ½ lb
1 tsp lemon juice
4 large / 450 g / 1 lb courgettes (zucchini)
1 medium onion, peeled and halved
4 tbsp / 50 g / 2 oz butter or margarine
salt and freshly ground pepper
2 tbsp / 25 g / 1 oz flour
2½ cups / 600 ml / 1 pint good chicken or vegetable stock
⅝ cup / 125 ml / ¼ pint single (light) cream
Garnish: chopped chives or parsley

Trim the fennel and quarter. Cook in boiling salted water with the lemon juice until tender – about 20 minutes. Drain thoroughly. While the fennel is cooking, slice the courgettes and onions using the slicing disc.

Heat the butter or margarine in a large pan and add the sliced vegetables with a little salt and pepper. Cover, and cook slowly for 15 minutes. Slice the drained fennel using the slicing disc and add to courgette mixture. Raise the heat and cook, stirring constantly for 1 minute, then stir in the flour followed by the stock. Bring to the boil, then cover and simmer for 20 minutes.

Strain the soup, reserving the liquid. Using the metal blade, process the vegetables until smooth. Return to the pan with the liquid and the cream. Reheat, adding more stock or water if the soup is too thick, and taste for seasoning. Sprinkle with the chopped chives or parsley just before serving.

FRESH TOMATO AND VODKA SOUP

*An unusual start for a dinner party, this soup is equally good
served hot or cold. If you really don't like vodka,
you can omit it, but the soup won't be quite the same.*

Serves 6
¾ cup / 75 g / 3 oz spring onions (scallions), trimmed
1 medium onion, peeled and quartered
1 small green chilli, seeded
1 clove garlic, peeled
2½ cups / 600 ml / 1 pint tomato juice
salt and freshly ground pepper
3 cups / 1 kg / 2 lbs ripe tomatoes, peeled and seeded
a little brown sugar
⅝ cup / 125 ml / ¼ pint vodka
Garnish: a few chopped chives

Cut the spring onions into thirds. Using the slicing disc,
slice the spring onions, onion, chilli and garlic. Put into a
large pan with half the tomato juice, and a little salt and
pepper. Cover and cook over low heat until the onions
are very soft – about 40 minutes.

Meanwhile, chop the tomatoes using the metal blade.
When the onions are soft, add the tomatoes to the pan
with a little brown sugar and the remaining tomato juice.
Cook uncovered, over medium heat for 20 minutes.
Strain the soup and reserve the liquid.

Using the metal blade, process the vegetables until
very smooth. Return to the liquid, and if the soup seems
too thin, reduce over high heat. Taste , and adjust the
seasoning. The soup can be served hot or chilled – either
way add the vodka and chives just before serving.

COUNTRY VEGETABLE SOUP

A hearty soup, full of natural goodness and flavour.

Serves 6
1 kg / 2 lbs mixed root vegetables – carrots, celery, Jerusalem artichokes, leeks, onions, parsnips, potatoes, swedes (rutabagas), turnips, etc.
2 cloves garlic, peeled
6 tbsp / 75 g / 3 oz butter or margarine
bayleaf
salt and pepper to taste
1¼ cups / 300 ml / ½ pint good chicken or vegetable stock
Garnish: a little grated cheese (optional)

Wash and prepare the vegetables, trimming and peeling where necessary. Cut the vegetables into pieces which will fit the feed tube, then, using the slicing disc, slice all the vegetables together with the garlic.

Heat the butter or margarine in a large pan and add the vegetables, bayleaf, and a little salt and pepper. Stir well, then cover and cook slowly for 15 minutes, stirring occasionally. Add the stock, bring to the boil, then cover and simmer gently for 30 minutes or until the vegetables are tender. Remove the bayleaf.

Strain the soup, reserving the liquid. Using the metal blade, process half the vegetables coarsely. Add to the liquid. Process the remaining vegetables until they form a thick purée. Add to the soup, reheat and taste for seasoning. Spoon into individual bowls and serve sprinkled with grated cheese, if wished.

CURRIED LENTIL SOUP

Serve with wholewheat bread and cheese to make a filling, nutritional meal.

Serves 4 to 6
¾ cup / 175 g / 6 oz lentils
2 medium onions, peeled
2 cloves garlic, peeled
2.5 cm / 1 inch piece root ginger, peeled
1 green chilli, seeded
2 stalks celery
1 red pepper, cored and seeded
4 medium tomatoes, peeled
⅔ cup / 110 g / 4 oz rindless, streaky bacon (optional)
2 tbsp oil
½ tsp ground coriander
½ tsp ground cumin
¼ tsp cayenne pepper, or to taste
5 cups / 1.15 litres / 2 pints chicken or vegetable stock
salt and freshly ground black pepper
Garnish: chopped fresh coriander leaves

Pick over the lentils, wash thoroughly and leave to drain. Using the metal blade, chop the onions with the garlic, ginger and chilli to form a thick paste. Scrape out of the bowl and reserve. Still using the metal blade, coarsely chop the celery, red pepper, tomatoes and bacon, if used.

Heat the oil in a heavy pan and quickly fry the ground coriander, cumin and cayenne pepper. After 5 seconds, add the onion paste and fry for a further 5 seconds. Add the tomato mixture and stir-fry for 1 minute.

Stir in the lentils, stock and salt and pepper to taste. Bring to the boil, then cover and simmer for about 40 minutes. Taste for seasoning, then stir in the fresh, chopped coriander. Serve very hot with warm, crusty bread and cheese.

QUICK CHILLED SUMMER SOUP

*Perfect for a meal on the patio, this soup can also be taken in
a thermos flask for summer picnics.*

Serves 4 to 6
1 large cucumber, peeled
2 ripe avocado pears, peeled
juice of ½ lime
1 tbsp fresh coriander leaves
1¼ cups / 300 ml / ½ pint plain yogurt, chilled
1¼ cups / 300 ml / ½ pint good chicken or vegetable stock, chilled
salt and pepper to taste
drop of Tabasco sauce
Garnish: lime slices and a few crushed ice cubes

Cut the cucumber into 5 cm / 2 inch chunks, and quarter
the avocados, discarding the stones. Using the metal
blade, process the cucumber and avocados with the lime
juice, coriander and yogurt, until very smooth. Tip into a
bowl and stir in the stock. Season to taste with salt,
pepper and a little Tabasco. If necessary, add a little more
lime juice, and if the soup is too thick, add a little milk,
stock or water.

Chill well. Just before serving, stir in a few crushed ice
cubes. Spoon into chilled bowls, and float lime slices on
the top.

Quick chilled Summer soup

A CARROT SOUP FROM GERMANY

Carrots, apples and onions may seem an odd combination, but this delicious soup is a traditional dish along the Rhine.

Serves 4 to 6
4 cups / 450 g / 1 lb carrots, peeled
bayleaf
4¼ cups / 1 litre / 1¾ pints good chicken stock
1 tsp brown sugar
3 medium onions, peeled and halved
1 large cooking apple, peeled and cored and quartered
6 tbsp / 75 g / 3 oz butter
salt and freshly ground pepper
a little lemon juice
Garnish: a little chopped chervil

Using the slicing disc, slice the carrots. Put into a large pan with the bayleaf, chicken stock, and brown sugar. Bring to a boil, then simmer until nearly tender.

Meanwhile, slice the onions and the apple using the slicing disc. Heat the butter in a frying pan, add the sliced onions and apple with a little salt and pepper. Fry until soft and golden brown. Add the contents of the frying pan to the carrots, and continue cooking until all the vegetables are very soft. Strain and reserve the liquid. Remove the bayleaf.

Using the metal blade, process the vegetable mixture until very smooth. Return to the liquid. Reheat and adjust the seasoning, adding a little lemon juice if necessary. Serve sprinkled with chopped chervil.

Carrot soup

ORIENTAL CHICKEN SOUP

Serve prawn or shrimp crackers with this slightly spicy, unusual soup.

Serves 6
2 chicken joints, skinned
2.5 cm / 1 inch piece root ginger, peeled
1 medium onion, peeled and quartered
4¼ cups / 1 litre / 1¾ pints good chicken or vegetable stock
1 large green pepper, cored, seeded and quartered
¼ cup / 25 g / 1 oz chinese egg noodles
soy sauce
freshly ground pepper
Garnish: – 2 spring (scallions) onions, sliced

Wipe the chicken joints and place in a large pan. Using the slicing disc, slice the ginger, and add the onion and ginger to the pan with the stock. Bring to the boil, then cover and simmer gently for 20 minutes, or until the chicken is very tender. Remove from the heat and allow to cool slightly. Remove the onion from the pan, then lift out and bone the chicken joints. Reserve the meat. Skim any fat from the liquid left in the pan.

Using the metal blade, coarsely chop the pepper. Add to the liquid in the pan. Using the same blade, finely chop the reserved chicken, and add to the pan with the noodles and a little soy sauce and ground pepper. Bring back to the boil, then simmer gently for 5 minutes. Taste for seasoning, and add a little more soya sauce if necessary. Spoon into individual bowls and garnish.

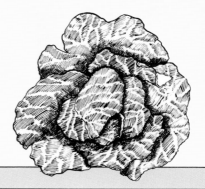

GAZPACHO

The basic soup is very smooth, and icy, and the guests add garnishes of their choice until the soup is very thick, and full of crunchy vegetables.

Serves 4 to 6
2¼ cups / 675 g / 1 ½ lbs ripe tomatoes, peeled and seeded
2 - 3 cloves garlic, peeled
6 slices crustless wholewheat bread, diced
1 green pepper, cored, seeded and quartered
1 red pepper, cored, seeded and quartered
4 tbsp good olive oil
4 tbsp red wine vinegar
1 large Spanish onion, peeled and quartered
1 large cucumber, peeled
2½ cups / 600 ml / 1 pint tomato juice
12 ice cubes
salt and freshly ground pepper
few drops Tabasco sauce
Garnishes: 1 small cucumber, peeled
1 red pepper, cored and seeded
1 green pepper, cored and seeded
6 spring onions, trimmed
2 tomatoes, peeled
garlic flavoured crôutons (optional)

Using the metal blade, process the tomatoes until smooth. With the machine still running, drop in the garlic, diced bread, peppers and gradually add the oil and vinegar. Cut the cucumber into 2.5 cm / 1 inch chunks and add with the onion to the mixture. Process until the soup is very smooth.

Tip into a bowl, stir in the tomato juice and ice cubes and season to taste with salt, pepper and Tabasco sauce. Chill until ready to serve.

Meanwhile, prepare the garnishes. Using the metal blade, coarsely chop each ingredient separately (except the crôutons). Put each of the garnishes into small bowls.

To serve: if the soup seems too thick, add more ice cubes. Spoon the soup into individual bowls. Arrange the bowls of vegetables and crôutons, if used, on a tray, so everyone can help themselves.

CHEESY ONION QUICHE

This is a favourite country recipe from Alsace.

Serves 6 to 8
Cheese Pastry: 1 cup / 100 g / 4 oz Cheddar cheese
1¼ cups / 150 g / 5 oz plain flour
6 tbsp / 75 g / 3 oz cold butter, diced
pinch each salt and cayenne pepper
1 egg, beaten
Filling: 6 cups / 675 g / 1½ lbs medium onions, peeled
6 tbsp / 75 g / 3 oz butter or margarine
salt and freshly ground pepper
bayleaf
⅝ cup / 150 ml / ¼ pint white wine
1 egg
3 tbsp whole milk
1 cup / 100 g / 4 oz Cheddar cheese

Set the oven at 375 F / 190 C / Gas 5.

First make the pastry. Using the grating disc, grate the cheese. Change to the metal blade and process the grated cheese with the flour, butter and seasonings, until the mixture resembles fine breadcrumbs. With the machine running, pour in the beaten egg, and process until the mixture forms a soft but not sticky dough. Turn out on to a floured surface and roll out fairly thickly, then use to line an 20 cm / 8 inch quiche dish. Bake blind in the heated oven for 10 to 15 minutes or until the pastry is looking golden and crisp.

While the pastry is cooking, prepare the filling. Using the slicing disc, slice the onions. Heat the butter or margarine in a large frying pan, then add the onions, a little salt and pepper, and the bayleaf. Fry over high heat, stirring constantly, until the onions are golden. Add the wine, and cook over medium heat, stirring frequently until all the liquid has evaporated. Remove the bayleaf. Mix the egg with the milk.

Spoon the onion mixture into the cooked pastry case, pressing the filling down well. Slice the cheese using the slicing disc, and arrange on top of the onions. Then carefully pour on the egg mixture. Place in the heated oven for 15 minutes or until the quiche is golden brown.

Serve hot, warm, or at room temperature.

AVOCADO AND BLUE CHEESE STARTER

*This makes a delicious start to a summer meal, but can also be
served as a light lunch for two. Again, Stilton can be
substituted with another mild blue cheese.*

Serves 4
¾ cup / 75 g / 3 oz Stilton or blue cheese, crumbled
4 tbs mayonnaise
4 tbs plain yogurt
½ tbs parsley sprigs
lemon juice to taste
freshly ground black pepper
3 ripe avocado pears, peeled
1 tbs walnut pieces
4 lettuce leaves

Using the metal blade, process the cheese with the
mayonnaise (see page 42), yogurt and parsley. Season to
taste with lemon juice and black pepper.

Halve each of the avocados. Remove the stones, scoop
out the flesh and retain the skins. Dice flesh and put into
a mixing bowl with the walnut pieces. Add the cheese
dressing and mix well.

Arrange each lettuce leaf on a small plate, and spoon
a portion of the avocado mixture back into four of
the skins.

EASY LIVER PATE

The contrast of textures makes this an unusual pâté, but it is an easy one to cook.

Serves 6 to 8
450 g / 1 lb chicken or duck livers
⅝ cup / 150 ml / ¼ pint milk
Marinade: ⅝ cup / 150 ml / pint brandy
1 tsp mixed spice
1 tsp ground black pepper
½ tsp fresh thyme
To cook: 4 tbsp / 50 g / 2 oz butter
1 shallot, peeled
½ cup / 75 g / 3 oz rindless streaky bacon
To finish: ½ cup / 50 g / 2 oz roasted hazelnuts
salt and freshly ground pepper
4 tbsp double whipping (heavy) cream, whipped
6 tbsp / 75 g / 3 oz butter, melted
bayleaf and sprig of thyme

Drain and trim the livers. Place in a china or glass bowl and pour over the milk. Cover and leave in the fridge for 2 to 3 hours. Drain off the milk and pat the livers dry.

Mix the brandy with the mixed spice, pepper and thyme, and add to the bowl of livers. Stir well, then cover and leave in the fridge overnight. Next day, remove the livers from the marinade, reserving the liquid, and pat dry.

Melt the butter in a medium-size, heavy pan. Using the metal blade, finely chop the shallot and the bacon. Add to the butter, and stir-fry over high heat until brown. Turn down the heat and carefully pour in the brandy marinade. Cover and simmer gently for 15 minutes.

Meanwhile, coarsely chop the roasted hazelnuts using the metal blade, and set aside.

When the livers are cooked, tip the contents of the pan into the processor bowl. Using the metal blade, process until the mixture forms a very smooth purée. Spoon into a bowl and stir in the hazelnuts. Taste for seasoning, and add a little salt and pepper if necessary.

Allow to cool, then stir in the whipped cream. Spoon into a terrine dish or other non-metallic container, and smooth the top. Pour over the melted butter and decorate with the bayleaf and thyme. Cover and chill until firm.

Serve with hot toast and butter.

Liver paté

KIPPER MOUSSE QUICHE

This luxurious quiche makes an easy first course for an elegant dinner, as well as travelling well for a picnic. As it is quite a rich dish, serve with lemon wedges and a cucumber salad.

Serves 6 to 8
Crunchy pastry: 1½ cups / 75 g / 3 oz cornflakes
¾ cup / 75 g / 3 oz plain flour
pinch each salt and pepper
6 tbsp / 75 g / 3 oz cold butter, diced
1 small egg, beaten
Filling: 450 g / 1 lb kipper fillets, cooked
1⅓ cups / 225 g / 8 oz cottage cheese with chives
a little lemon juice
freshly ground black pepper
⅝ cup / 150 ml / ¼ pint double (heavy) cream, whipped
Garnish: lemon slices

Set the oven at 375 F / 190 C / Gas 5.

First make the pastry. Using the metal blade, process the cornflakes, flour, salt and pepper and butter, until the mixture resembles breadcrumbs. With the machine running, pour in the beaten egg, and process until the mixture forms a soft but not sticky dough. Turn out on to a well floured board and roll out fairly thickly. Use to line an 20 cm / 8 inch oven-proof china quiche dish. Bake blind in the heated oven for 10 to 15 minutes or until the pastry is crisp and golden brown. Allow to cool completely.

Meanwhile make the filling. Skin and flake the cooled, cooked kipper fillets. Using the metal blade, process the cottage cheese until smooth. Add the flaked fish with the lemon juice and black pepper. Process until very smooth and light. Fold this mixture into the whipped cream. Taste for seasoning, adding more lemon juice and pepper if necessary. Spoon mixture into the pastry case and chill well.

Garnish the quiche with lemon slices, and serve well-chilled with lemon wedges and a cucumber salad.

QUICK BLUE CHEESE PATE

*If Stilton is not available use any other mild blue cheese such
as Roquefort or Danish Blue.*

Serves 4
2 cups / 225 g / 8 oz Stilton or Blue cheese, crumbled
4 tbsp / 50 g / 2 oz unsalted butter, softened
2 tbsp port
3 tbsp mayonnaise
freshly ground black pepper
Garnish: 4 pecan halves

Using the metal blade, process the cheese with the butter
and the port until smooth. Quickly mix in the mayonnaise (see page 42) and a little pepper. Taste for seasoning, then spoon into four small individual dishes. Press a
pecan on top of each, then cover and chill.

Serve with hot toast and a watercress salad.

ASPARAGUS AND EGG NAPOLEON

This is a kind of mille-feuille made with a quick rough-puff pastry, and filled with asparagus and scrambled egg. The pastry can be made several days in advance and crisped up before use. For a change, replace the asparagus with strips of smoked salmon, cooked smoked haddock, or kipper fillets.

Serves 6
Pastry: 3¼ cups / 350 g / 12 oz plain flour
large pinch salt
½ cup / 100 g / 4 oz cold butter or block margarine
½ cup / 100 g / 4 oz cold lard or vegetable fat
approx. 7 tbsp icy water
3 tsp lemon juice
beaten egg to glaze
Filling: 24 spears cooked asparagus (fresh or canned)
6 tbsp / 75 g / 3 oz butter
9 eggs
⅝ cup / 150 ml / ¼ pint single (light) or double (heavy) cream
salt and freshly ground pepper

Set the oven at 400 F / 200 C / Gas 6.

First make the pastry. Using the metal blade, mix the flour with the salt. Cut the fats into 2.5 cm / 1 inch cubes and add to the flour. Process briefly, until the fats become thumb-nail size flakes. Tip into a mixing bowl and stir in the water and lemon juice using a round-bladed knife, adding more water if needed. (This can also be done in the processor, using the plastic blade, but it needs practice.) You should have a soft but not sticky, lumpy-looking dough. Wrap well and chill for about 30 minutes.

Sprinkle a work surface and rolling pin with flour, and carefully roll out the dough to a rectangle 38 cm × 13 cm / 15 inches × 5 inches. Fold the top third of the pastry down and the bottom third of the pastry up to make a three-layered square of pastry. Turn the pastry so the fold is on your left, and roll and fold the pastry as before. Wrap and chill for 15 minutes. Repeat the rolling, folding and chilling procedure twice more, so the pastry has been folded a total of 6 times.

Grease 2 large baking sheets. Roll out the pastry to a rectangle 35 cm × 23 cm / 14 inches × 9 inches (or the length of your baking sheets), and 3 mm / ⅛th inch thick. Cut the rectangle in half to make 2 thin rectangles 35 cm / 14 inches long. Place on the baking sheets and prick well. Brush with beaten egg, then bake in the heated oven until golden and crispy – about 10 minutes. Cool on a wire rack, then trim off the edges, and cut each sheet into 6 strips.

When ready to eat – gently warm the pastry and the asparagus tips. Melt the butter in a heavy pan. Using the plastic blade, process the eggs till frothy with half the cream and a little salt and plenty of pepper. Tip into the pan and stir over low heat until the eggs are lightly scrambled. Remove from the heat and taste for seasoning. Stir in the rest of the cream. Place a strip of pastry on each of 6 plates. Divide the scrambled eggs between the pastry bases, then arrange 4 spears of asparagus on top of each. Cover with remaining pastry strips. Serve straight away.

CRUNCHY PEPPER AND TUNA MOUSSE

Set in a Tupperware or plastic container instead of a glass
bowl, this tangy, textured mousse makes a picnic treat.

Serves 6
1 cup / 225 g / 8 oz can tuna, drained
2 hard-boiled eggs
1 red pepper, cored and seeded
1 green pepper, cored and seeded
1 tbs / 15 g / ½ oz butter or margarine
2 tsp / 15 g / ½ oz flour
⅝ cup / 150 ml / ¼ pint whole milk
3 tbs water
2 tsp / 11 g / ¼ oz gelatine
⅝ cup / 150 ml / ¼ pint mayonnaise
⅝ cup / 150 ml / ¼ pint double (heavy) cream, whipped
2 tbs lemon juice
salt and freshly ground pepper
tomato ketchup, to taste (optional)
Garnish: lemon slices or pepper rings

Using the metal blade, process the tuna until coarsely
mashed. Tip into a mixing bowl. Using the same blade,
coarsely chop the eggs, and add to the tuna. In the same
way coarsely chop the peppers (they should be the size of
your little finger-nail) and mix into the tuna and eggs.

Melt the butter in a small pan, and stir in the flour
followed by the milk. Bring to the boil, stirring constantly. Simmer for two minutes. Tip on to a large plate
and allow the sauce to cool completely.

Meanwhile, put the water into a small pan and
sprinkle in the gelatine. Leave to soak for 5 minutes, then
gently melt over low heat.

Mix the cooled sauce into the tuna mixture with the
melted gelatine, mayonnaise, and whipped cream.
Season to taste with lemon juice, salt and pepper and
tomato ketchup, if used.

Spoon into a glass bowl, cover and chill until firm.
Garnish with thin lemon slices or pepper rings, and
serve with a green salad and crusty bread.

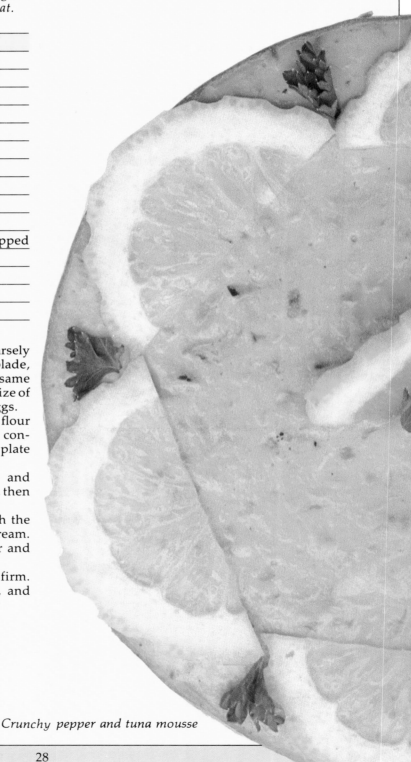

Crunchy pepper and tuna mousse

HERBY ROULADE

This impressive dish can be served as a dinner party first course, or as a main dish with cold meats and baked potatoes.

Serves 6
Roulade: ½ cup / 50 g / 2 oz Cheddar cheese
⅓ cup / 50 g / 2 oz Parmesan cheese
1 cup / 50 g / 2 oz crustless brown bread, diced
⅝ cup / 150 ml / ¼ pint sour cream
3 tbsp whole milk
1 tbsp parsley
1 tbsp snipped chives
1 tbsp chervil
4 eggs, separated
salt and freshly ground pepper
Filling: 3 tbsp mayonnaise
4 large lettuce leaves
2 tbsp olive oil
1 tsp wine vinegar
salt and freshly ground pepper
French mustard to taste
1 tbsp basil leaves, chopped
4 tomatoes, peeled, quartered and seeded

Set the oven at 400 F / 200 C / Gas 6.

Grease a Swiss roll tin (jelly-roll pan) 33 × 23 cm / 13 × 9 inches and line with greaseproof or waxed paper.

Using the grating disc, grate the Cheddar and Parmesan. Tip into a mixing bowl. Using the metal blade process the diced bread into fine crumbs. Using the same blade process the grated cheeses, breadcrumbs, cream, milk, herbs and egg yolks. Whip the egg whites until stiff and mix in quickly. Add salt and pepper to taste.

Spoon into the prepared tin and bake in the heated oven for 10 minutes, or until firm and golden. Remove from the oven and cover with a damp, clean tea-towel and leave to cool.

Turn out the roulade on to a sheet of non-stick baking paper and trim the edges. Spread the roulade with the mayonnaise and cover with lettuce leaves. Using the metal blade, quickly process the oil with the vinegar, salt, pepper, mustard and basil until smooth.

Arrange the tomatoes on the lettuce leaves. Spoon over the basil dressing, and roll up the roulade like a Swiss roll. Serve immediately.

SALADS AND VEGETABLES

Jansson's Temptation 32

Spicy Potatoes 33

Five Vegetable Gratin 34

Cheesy Ratatouille 35

Vegetable Chop Suey 36

Crispy Fried Cabbage 37

Potato Supper 38

Lentil Purée 39

Nutty Rice Pilau 40

Beetroot, Apple Roquefort and Walnut Salad 41

Mayonnaise 42

Vinaigrette 43

Warm Potato and Bacon Salad 44

Provençal Rice Salad 45

Fennel Salad 46

Curried Coleslaw 47

Rainbow Salad 47

JANSSON'S TEMPTATION

This is the famous potato and anchovy gratin from Sweden.
Starting the potatoes off in milk helps
prevent the cream from curdling.

Serves 4 to 6
1 kg / 2 lbs potatoes, peeled
2½ cups / 600 ml / 1 pint milk
450 g /1 lb onions, peeled
2-3 cloves garlic
1¼ cups / 300 ml / ½ pint soured cream
2 × (50 g / 1¾ oz) cans anchovy fillets
salt and freshly ground black pepper
4 tbsp / 50 g / 2 oz butter
Set the oven at 400 F / 200 C / Gas 6.

Slice the potatoes using the slicing disc. Place in a large pan with the milk. Cover and simmer gently for 10 minutes or until the potatoes are half-cooked. Drain off the milk, which can be used in soups.

While the potatoes are cooking, slice the onions and garlic using the slicing disc.

Gently mix the half-cooked potatoes with the onions, garlic and half the cream. Drain the oil from the anchovies and add with plenty of pepper – salt may not be necessary if the anchovies are very salty. Use half the butter to grease an oven-proof baking dish. Spoon half the potato mixture into the baking dish and arrange the anchovy fillets evenly on top, then cover with the remaining potato mixture. Dot with the rest of the butter and bake in the heated oven for 35 minutes, or until golden brown and bubbling. Pour over the remaining cream and serve immediately.

SPICY POTATOES

You can make this dish as spicy or as mild as you like. In any case these potatoes are wonderful served with sausages, chops or curries.

Serves 4 to 6
1 kg / 2 lbs large potatoes, peeled and quartered
6 tbsp oil
4 tbsp / 50 g / 2 oz butter
3 cloves garlic, peeled
2.5 cm / 1 inch piece of root ginger, peeled and sliced
3 tsp mustard seeds
½ tsp turmeric
1½ tsp chilli powder, or to taste
1½ tsp coarse sea salt, or to taste
freshly ground black pepper
½ tsp ground coriander
1 - 2 tbsp fresh coriander or mint leaves

Slice the potatoes using the slicing disc.

Heat the oil and butter in a large heavy frying pan. Add the garlic and ginger and fry for 2 minutes or until browned. Remove using a slotted spoon. Add the mustard seeds and fry for a couple of minutes. When the seeds begin to pop, add the potatoes and carefully stir-fry for 1 minute. Sprinkle over the turmeric, chilli powder, sea-salt, pepper and ground coriander. Mix in well, then fry the potatoes over medium-high heat, turning frequently, for about 10 minutes, until crisp and golden brown.

Meanwhile, chop the coriander or mint using the metal blade. When the potatoes are ready to serve, stir in the herbs, taste for seasoning and spoon into a warmed serving dish.

FIVE VEGETABLE GRATIN

This is a nutritious and hearty main dish, that can be prepared in advance. It makes a lovely winter supper.

Serves 4 as a main dish, or 6 as a first course.
Base: 8 cups / 1 kg / 2 lbs onions, peeled and halved
4 cups / 450 g / 1 lb leeks, trimmed
4 tbsp / 50 g / 2 oz butter or margarine
6 tbsp / 40 g / 1½ oz flour
1⅞ cups / 450 ml / ¾ pint milk
1 cup / 100 g / 4 oz Gruyère or strong Cheddar cheese
salt and freshly ground pepper
a pinch of nutmeg
Middle: 6 eggs
½ cup / 50 g / 2 oz Gruyère or strong Cheddar cheese
Topping: 3 cups / 275 g / 10 oz each carrots, parsnips, potatoes, all peeled
4 tbsp / 50 g / 2 oz butter
1 tbsp snipped chives or parsley (optional)
salt and pepper to taste
½ cup / 50 g / 2 oz Gruyère or strong Cheddar cheese
Set the oven at 400 F / 200 C / Gas 6.

Using the slicing disc slice the onions. Reserve. Rinse and slice the leeks, using the same disc. Steam or boil the leeks until just tender, and set aside. Drain.

Melt the butter or margarine in a large pan. Stir in the onions and cook slowly till soft and golden, about 15 to 20 minutes. Take pan off the heat, stir in the flour, then gradually stir in the milk. Return to the heat and stir continuously until the mixture comes to the boil. Simmer for 2 minutes.

Meanwhile, using the grating disc grate all the cheese needed for the whole recipe (2 cups / 200 g / 8 oz in all).

Stir the leeks and 1 cup / 100 g / 4 oz of the grated cheese into the sauce, and season to taste. Spoon into a large shallow, greased baking dish. Make 6 hollows in the mixture for the eggs, and allow to cool. Break an egg into each hollow, and sprinkle ½ cup / 50 g / 2 oz of the grated cheese over the eggs.

While the base is cooling, roughly chop the carrots, parsnips and potatoes and steam or boil until tender. Drain, if necessary, then using the metal blade, process with the butter, herbs and seasoning until very smooth and creamy. You may have to do this in two batches. Taste for seasoning.

If you are preparing the dish in advance, allow the topping to cool before spooning carefully over the eggs and onion mixture in the baking dish. Smooth the top.

When ready to cook – sprinkle the remaining ½ cup / 50 g / 2 oz grated cheese over the topping. Bake in the heated oven for 15 to 20 minutes until brown and bubbling. The exact timing will depend on how you like your eggs cooked, and whether the gratin has come straight from the fridge, or has been prepared immediately beforehand.

CHEESY RATATOUILLE

A lovely, colourful dish which can be served as a first course,
or as a main course with
baked potatoes, or as a vegetable accompaniment.

Serves 4 to 6
3 medium onions, peeled
4 tbsp olive oil
2 medium aubergines (egg plant), halved
450 g / 1 lb courgettes (zucchini), trimmed
1 large red pepper, cored, seeded and halved
1 large green pepper, cored, seeded and halved
1 large yellow pepper, cored, seeded and halved
3 cloves garlic, peeled
450 g / 1 lb ripe tomatoes, quartered
salt and freshly ground pepper
ground coriander to taste
1 tsp thyme
1 cup / 100 g / 4 oz Cheddar cheese
topping: 2 tbsp breadcrumbs
2 tbsp grated Parmesan cheese
1 cup / 100 g / 4 oz Cheddar cheese

Halve the onions and slice using the slicing disc. Heat the oil in a large, deep, heavy pan, add the onions, and cook over medium heat for 5 minutes.

While the onions are cooking, slice the aubergines, using the slicing disc. Sprinkle with a little salt, mix well, and place in a colander to drain for 5 minutes. Rinse well and pat dry with paper towels.

Using the slicing disc, slice the courgettes, peppers and garlic. Add the sliced vegetables and quartered tomatoes to the pan. Stir well over high heat for a minute then stir in salt, pepper, thyme and ground coriander to taste. Cook, stirring frequently, over medium high heat for 20 minutes or until the vegetables are just tender. If there is too much liquid, turn up the heat, and boil rapidly till reduced – the ratatouille should be fairly dry. Taste the ratatouille, it should be well seasoned.

Grate all the cheese (both for the ratatouille and the topping) using the grating disc. Heat the grill (broiler). Stir half the grated cheese (1 cup / 100 g / 4 oz) into the vegetable mixture, and transfer to a greased oven-proof baking dish. Mix the ingredients for the topping together and sprinkle over the ratatouille. Grill until golden brown and bubbling.

SALADS
AND VEGETABLES

VEGETABLE CHOP SUEY

Root ginger adds a fresh spiciness.

Serves 4
2 large carrots, peeled
1 medium leek, trimmed
2 medium onions, peeled
227 g / 8 oz can bamboo shoots
2.5 cm / 1 inch piece root ginger, peeled
1¾ cups / 100 g / 4 oz button mushrooms
2¼ cups / 175 g /6 oz beansprouts
2 tbsp oil for frying
1 tsp cornflour (cornstarch)
⅝ cup / 150 ml / ¼ pint vegetable stock
3 tbsp tomato ketchup
½ - 1 tbsp soy sauce, to taste
salt to taste
Garnish: 6 spring onions (scallions), trimmed

First prepare all the vegetables for cooking. Use either the julienne disc or coarse grating disc to shred the carrots. Set aside. Halve the leek and rinse well. Halve the onions, then slice with the leek using the slicing disc.

Set aside. Drain the bamboo shoots and slice in the same way. Set aside. Slice the spring onions using the same disc, and set aside. Use the grating disc to grate the ginger. Quarter the mushrooms. Put the beansprouts in a colander and pour 2½ cups / 600 ml / 1 pint boiling water over them. Drain thoroughly.

Heat the oil in a wok or large, deep, frying pan. Add the ginger, carrots, and onions. Stir-fry for 2 minutes then stir in the leeks, bamboo shoots and mushrooms. Stir-fry over high heat for 2 minutes, then stir in the beansprouts, and fry for 1 minute. Mix the cornflour with the stock, ketchup and soy sauce. Stir into the vegetables and bring to the boil, stirring constantly. When the mixture has thickened taste for seasoning, adding more soy sauce, ketchup or salt if necessary. Transfer the chop suey to a warmed serving dish and sprinkle with the spring onions.

Variation: For a non-vegetarian chop suey, add ¾ cup -1½ cups / 100 g to 225 g / 4 oz to 8 oz shelled shrimps, or diced cooked chicken to the chop suey with the bamboo shoots and mushrooms.

CRISPY FRIED CABBAGE

Even children will eat cabbage cooked this way. Serve with grilled or fried meat, sausages or bacon.

Serves 4 to 6
1 small, firm green or white cabbage
1 medium onion, peeled
2 tbsp oil
4 tbsp / 50 g / 2 oz butter
1 tbsp caraway seeds
sea salt and freshly ground pepper

Trim the cabbage, removing the outer leaves and core. Quarter and shred the cabbage using the coleslaw, or slicing disc. Wash in icy water, then drain. Halve and slice the onion using the slicing disc.

Heat the oil and butter in a heavy sauté pan, deep frying pan, or wok. When very hot, stir in the cabbage, onion and caraway seeds. Stir-fry for 2 to 3 minutes until crisp and brown. Add salt and pepper to taste. Turn into a warmed serving dish and serve immediately.

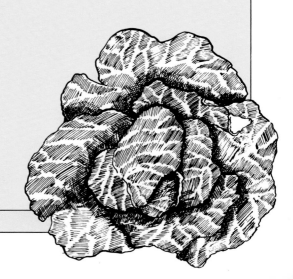

POTATO SUPPER

A processor makes this dish in a matter of minutes. Serve with a crisp green salad for a complete meal.

Serves 4 to 6
1 cup / 175 g / 6 oz back (Canadian) bacon
1 kg / 2 lb potatoes, peeled
1 cup / 100 g / 4 oz Cheddar cheese
2 cloves garlic, peeled
3 eggs
1¼ cups / 300 ml / ½ pint soured cream
6 spring onions (scallions), trimmed
1 tbsp parsley
salt and freshly ground pepper
Set the oven at 400 F / 200 C / Gas 6.

Heat the grill (broiler), then grill the bacon until crisp. Drain on paper towels.

Coarsely grate the potatoes using the grating disc or coleslaw disc. Remove the excess water from the potatoes by squeezing well, then draining on paper towels. Grate the cheese using the grating disc. Set aside.

Put the garlic, cream, eggs, quartered spring onions and parsley sprigs into the processor fitted with the metal blade. Process until the onions and parsley are finely chopped. Crumble the bacon, add to the machine and process for a couple of seconds. Mix the grated potatoes with the grated cheese in a bowl, then stir in the egg and cream mixture. Season to taste, then pour into a greased shallow oven-proof baking dish.

Place in the heated oven and bake for 30 to 40 minutes until golden brown and crispy.

Potato supper

LENTIL PUREE

*This German dish is best served with ham, pork,
or game dishes.*

Serves 4
1 cup / 225 g /8 oz lentils
2½ cups / 600 ml / 1 pint vegetable or chicken stock
⅔ cup / 100 g / 4 oz Polish-style garlic sausage or smoked sausage
1 large onion, peeled
2 cloves garlic, peeled
1 bouquet garni
4 tbsp / 50 g / 2 oz butter
4 tbsp double (heavy) cream
2 tbsp fresh herbs – parsley, chives, chervil savoury
salt and freshly ground pepper

Rinse the lentils and pick over. Place in a pan with the stock. Peel the sausage if necessary, and add to the pan. Slice the onion and garlic, using the slicing disc. Add to the pan with the bouquet garni. Cover, bring to a boil, and simmer for about 40 minutes, until a thick purée has been formed.

Remove the bouquet garni and discard. Remove the sausage and chop roughly. Put the lentils and sausage in the processor fitted with the metal blade, and process until smooth. With the machine running, gradually add the butter, cream and herbs. Taste for seasoning, then spoon into a warmed serving dish.

NUTTY RICE PILAU

This is a complete main dish, but can be served as a first course or as an accompaniment.

Serves 6 as a main dish
1 large onion, peeled and quartered
2¼ cups / 175 g / 6 oz mushrooms
2 tbsp oil
2¼ cups / 450 g /1 lb long-grain American rice
1¼ cups / 298 g / 10½ oz can condensed consommé soup
600 ml / 1 pint water
bouquet garni
¾ cup / 75 g / 3 oz hazelnuts
⅓ cup / 50 g / 2 oz almonds
½ cup / 50 g /2 oz walnuts
2 tbsp / 25 g / 1 oz pine nuts
1 tbsp sunflower seeds
4 tbsp / 50 g / 2 oz butter
salt and freshly ground pepper
Garnish: 1 tbsp snipped chives, 1 tbsp sesame seeds

Set the oven at 350 F / 180 C / Gas 4.

Using the metal blade, coarsely chop the onion. Add the mushrooms and process for about 10 seconds, or until the onions and mushrooms are evenly chopped into medium-sized pieces.

Heat the oil in an oven-proof casserole, add the onion mixture and fry over medium heat for a couple of minutes. Add the rice and fry for a minute or until golden. Stir in the consommé, water and bouquet garni. Bring to the boil then stir well, cover, and place in the oven. Cook for 20 to 25 minutes, without stirring.

While the rice is cooking, toast the hazelnuts and almonds in the oven until golden brown. Put into the processor with the walnuts, pine nuts and sunflower seeds. Using the metal blade, process for a couple of seconds, to chop coarsely.

When the rice is tender and all the liquid has been absorbed, remove the bouquet garni, and stir in the nuts, butter and seasonings. Sprinkle with the chives, and sesame seeds, and serve piping hot.

Variation 1: Replace half of the quantity of nuts with grated cheese.

Variation 2: Replace the condensed consommé soup with condensed tomato soup.

Nutty rice pilau

BEETROOT, APPLE ROQUEFORT AND WALNUT SALAD

A very attractive salad to serve with cold meats and baked jacket potatoes on a chilly day.

Serves 4
450 g / 1 lb beetroot (beets) boiled and peeled
5 tablespoons vinaigrette (page 00)
2 crisp green apples, quartered and cored
½ crisp lettuce, rinsed
¾ cup / 75 g / 3 oz Roquefort cheese
½ cup / 50 g / 2 oz walnut halves

Trim the beetroot, and halve if necessary. Shred using the julienne or coleslaw disc, or chop into finger-nail sized pieces using the metal blade. Turn into a bowl and mix with half the vinaigrette.

Rinse out the processor bowl and slice the apples using the metal bowl. Turn into a clean bowl and toss with the remaining dressing.

Tear up the lettuce and arrange in a salad bowl. Arrange the beetroot on top, then the apple slices. Crumble the cheese over the whole salad and decorate with the walnut halves.

MAYONNAISE

Use this recipe as the basis for many interesting and delicious sauces and dressings.

Makes approx. 1¼ cups / 300 ml / ½ pint
3 egg yolks
½ tsp mustard powder
salt and pepper
½ - 1 tbsp white wine vinegar
⅝ cup / 150 ml / ¼ pint sunflower or safflower oil
⅝ cup / 150 ml / ¼ pint olive oil
1 tbsp hot water

Using the metal blade, process the egg yolks with the mustard powder, a little salt and pepper and ½ tbsp of vinegar till well mixed. With the machine running, add the oil, drop by drop, through the feed tube. The mixture should become very thick and emulsified. Taste for seasoning, adding more salt, pepper and vinegar as necessary. Finally, with the machine running, pour the hot water in through the feed tube.

Store the mayonnaise in a glass or china bowl, cover and chill.

Variations
1 Curry mayonnaise: add 2 - 3 tsp curry paste (or to taste), plus 2 tsp mango, apricot, or ginger chutney, and a few chopped fresh coriander leaves to the mayonnaise with the hot water. Serve with hard-boiled eggs, prawns (shrimps), or cold poultry.
2 Green Mayonnaise: chop 1 cup / 100 g / 4 oz watercress using the metal blade. Add to the mayonnaise with the water. Serve with hard-boiled eggs, cold cooked asparagus or globe artichokes, or cold roast veal or pork.
3 Watercress Mousseline: chop 1 cup / 100 g / 4 oz watercress using the metal blade. Mix with ⅝ cup / 150 ml / ¼ pint of the made mayonnaise. Whip ⅝ cup / 150 ml / ¼ pint of double (whipping) cream and stir in. Taste for seasoning. Serve with cold poached fish – salmon, sole, prawns, shrimps or lobster, or cold roast chicken.
4 Marie-Rose Mayonnaise: mix 2 to 3 tbsp tomato ketchup and a couple of drops of Tabasco sauce and add to the mayonnaise with the water. Serve with prawns, shrimps, crab, lobster, fish croquettes, fish cakes or egg salads.
5 Garlic and Herb Mayonnaise: chop ½ tbsp each parsley sprigs, tarragon leaves, basil leaves and snipped chives, with 1 to 2 cloves garlic using the metal blade. Add to the mayonnaise with the water. Serve with cold cooked vegetables and salads, or as a dip.

6 Yogurt Mayonnaise: mix ⅝ cup / 150 ml / ¼ pint of plain thick yogurt with ⅝ cup / 150 ml / ¼ pint of the mayonnaise, and 1 to 2 tbsp snipped chives. Season to taste. Serve with avocados, asparagus, globe artichokes, cold poached fish, green salads and raw vegetables.
7 Soured Cream Mayonnaise: mix ⅝ cup / 150 ml / ¼ pint soured cream with an equal quantity of the mayonnaise. Season to taste. (Use the metal blade to chop ½ tbsp mint and 3 tbsp cucumber and add to mayonnaise). Or replace the cucumber with 2 tbsp chopped spring onions (scallions). Serve as a dip, or with salads.
8 Tartare Sauce: using the metal blade, chop 2 tbsp each capers and gherkins and parsley sprigs. Add to the mayonnaise with the hot water. Serve with fried fish of savoury fritters.
9 Avocado Mayonnaise: using the metal blade, process ⅝ cup / 150 ml / ¼ pint of the mayonnaise with an equal quantity of plain thick yogurt, a tsp of lemon juice and a ripe avocado, peeled and diced. Season to taste with salt and cayenne pepper. Serve as a dip, or with green salads and seafood.
10 Egg and Chive Mayonnaise: add 2 shelled hard-boiled eggs and 2 tbsp snipped chives to the mayonnaise with the hot water. Serve with green salads and vegetables or with cold fish or shellfish.

VINAIGRETTE

This is a basic salad dressing. Below are some tasty variations to liven up the most simple salad.

Makes approximately ⅔ cup / 175 ml / 6 fl oz
4 tbsp olive or walnut oil
4 tbsp safflower or sunflower oil
2 tablespoons wine or sherry vinegar
½ teaspoon sea salt
½ teaspoon freshly ground black pepper
½ - 1 teaspoon mustard powder

Process all the ingredients together using the metal blade or plastic blade, until emulsified. Taste for seasoning.
Variations
1 Herbed Vinaigrette: chop 2 tablespoons fresh herbs – parsley, chives, tarragon, mint, basil, etc, using the metal blade. Stir into the vinaigrette.
2 Garlic Vinaigrette: place all the ingredients for the vinaigrette in the processor, and process using the metal blade. While the machine is running, drop 1 to 3 peeled cloves of garlic in through the feed tube.
3 Roquefort Dressing: place all the ingredients for the vinaigrette, except the salt, in the processor, and process using the metal blade. While the machine is running, add ½ cup / 50 g / 2 oz crumble Roquefort cheese, 2 tsp lemon juice. When the mixture has emulsified, taste for seasoning .
4 Egg and Herb Vinaigrette: add 1 egg yolk to the ingredients, and process using the metal blade. When the mixture has emulsified, add 2 shelled, quartered hard-boiled eggs, 1 tablespoon fresh herbs (parsley, chives, thyme, tarragon, basil, dill, etc), and process for 5 seconds. Taste for seasoning.
5 Chilli Vinaigrette: add 1 to 2 green chilli peppers, seeded, cored and quartered, to the ingredients before processing. Or add 1 to 2 crumbled dried red chillis and a few sesame seeds to the ingredients before processing.
6 Cream Dressing: using the metal blade, process equal quantities of mayonnaise and vinaigrette. Add a few snipped chives, and season to taste, using a couple of drops of Tabasco sauce, if wished.

WARM POTATO AND BACON SALAD

Serve as a first course, or with cold poultry or quiches.

Serves 4
450 g / 1 lb small new potatoes, scrubbed
3 tablespoons olive oil
1⅓ cups / 225 g / 8 oz streaky bacon
1 medium onion, peeled and quartered
4 tablespoons wine vinegar
5 tablespoons chicken or beef stock
salt and freshly ground pepper
sugar to taste
2 egg yolks, beaten
1 tablespoon fresh, sipped dill

Cook the potatoes in boiling salted water for about 20 minutes or until tender. Drain and turn into a oven-proof serving dish.

Meanwhile, chop the bacon and onion into medium-size pieces using the metal blade. Heat the oil in a deep frying pan. Add the bacon and onion and fry gently for 5 minutes to soften the onion. Turn up the heat and fry until the bacon becomes crispy.

Remove from the heat, and add the vinegar and stock. Bring to the boil then taste, and season. Remove from the heat and stir in the egg yolks and dill. Pour over the potatoes and toss well. Serve immediately.

PROVENCAL RICE SALAD

*A meal in itself, serve with red wine and crusty french bread
for a taste of the Mediterranean.*

Serves 4
1⅓ cups / 225 / 8 oz long grain rice, cooked
8 spring onions (scallions), trimmed
2 cups / 225 g / 8 oz French beans, cooked
3 hard-boiled eggs, shelled
1¼ cups / 184 g / 6½ oz can tuna, drained
½ cup / 50 g / 2 oz black olives, stoned
garlic and anchovy dressing:
2 - 3 cloves garlic, peeled
4 anchovy fillets
1 egg yolk
¾ cup / 175 ml / 6 fl oz vinaigrette (page 43)
salt and freshly ground pepper
Garnish: fresh coriander leaves

Put the rice in a large bowl and toss with a fork to
separate the grains. Slice the spring onions using the
slicing disc, and add to the rice.

Using the metal blade, coarsely chop the fresh beans
and add to the rice with the quartered eggs. Flake the
tuna and add with the olives.

For the dressing, put the garlic, anchovies and egg yolk
in the processor bowl fitted with the metal blade. Process
for a couple of seconds. With the machine running, pour
in the vinaigrette through the feed tube. Process until
smooth and emulsified. Pour over the rice mixture and
toss well. Taste for seasoning, adding more salt and
pepper if necessary. Leave to stand for 20 to 30 minutes,
then spoon into a salad bowl and garnish with the
coriander leaves.

FENNEL SALAD

*A sharp, tangy salad, that is refreshingly served with
cold meat pies, or rich mousses.*

Serves 6
3 heads fennel, trimmed
2 medium courgettes (zucchini)
1½ cups / 100 g / 4 oz beansprouts
1 cup / 100 g / 4 oz watercress
Lemon and herb dressing:
grated rind of ½ lemon
3 tablespoons lemon juice
4 tablespoons olive oil
¼ teaspoon mustard powder
salt and freshly ground black pepper
1 tablespoon snipped chives or parsley sprigs

Using the slicing disc, slice the fennel. Plunge into a
bowl of icy water. Leave for 5 minutes, or until crisp,
then drain thoroughly.

Meanwhile, slice the courgettes using the slicing disc.
Pick over the beansprouts and watercress.

Mix the fennel with the courgettes, beansprouts and
watercress.

For the dressing, combine all the ingredients and process using the metal blade for 5 to 10 seconds or until
emulsified. Taste for seasoning, then pour over the salad
and toss well.

Rainbow salad

RAINBOW SALAD

A colourful salad to cheer up a winter's day.

Serves 6 to 8
3 cups / 225 g / 8 oz red cabbage, trimmed and cored
3 cups / 225 g / 8 oz white cabbage, trimmed and cored
2 medium courgettes (zucchini), trimmed
2 large carrots, peeled
1 medium onion, peeled
2 green-skinned apples, cored and quartered
⅝ cup / 300 ml / ½ pint Yogurt Mayonnaise (page 42) or Soured Cream Mayonnaise (page 42)
salt and freshly ground pepper
Garnish: 1 tablespoon pomegranate seeds (optional)

Using the coleslaw disc, grating disc, or slicing disc, shred the cabbage, courgettes, carrots, onion and apples. Put into a large bowl and toss well with the mayonnaise. Taste, and add salt and pepper if necessary. Spoon into a salad bowl and sprinkle with the pomegranate seeds.

CURRIED COLESLAW

This crisp salad is a refreshing change from the usual ubiquitous, bland coleslaw.

Serves 4
3 cups / 225 g / 8 oz white cabbage, trimmed and cored
2 medium carrots, peeled
1 large green-skinned apple
4 spring onions (scallions), trimmed
⅝ cup / 150 ml / ¼ curry mayonnaise (page 42)
⅓ cup / 50 g / 2 oz cashew nuts or dry-roasted peanuts
salt and freshly ground pepper
Garnish: coriander leaves

Using the coleslaw disc, grating disc, or slicing disc, shred the cabbage and carrots. Turn into a mixing bowl. Using the slicing disc, slice the apples and onions.

Add to the cabbage and carrots with the mayonnaise and nuts. Toss well and taste for seasoning. Spoon into a salad bowl and garnish with coriander leaves.

Variation: add shredded chicken, diced ham, prawns or shrimps to the salad for a main dish.

MEAT AND POULTRY

Swedish Meatballs with Soured Cream and Dill Sauce 50

Vitello Tonnato *51*

Liver Stroganoff *52*

Corned Beef Stuffed Potatoes *54*

Stir-Fried Beef with Baby Corn and Green Peppers *55*

Chinese Chicken with Pineapple and Cashew Nuts *56*

Fried Pork with Mushrooms and Water Chestnuts *57*

Sauté of Lamb with Cranberries *58*

Spiced Lamb and Cheese Meatloaf *59*

Stuffed Cabbage Leaves *60*

Curry-Fried Turkey *61*

Pork Dijonnaise *62/63*

Lamb with Fennel and Lemon Sauce *64*

Pheasant Pojarski Crôutes *65*

Mushroom Sauce *66*

Chicken Stuffed with Fruit and Nuts *67*

Hot Game Pie with Fried Apples and Onions *68/69*

Duck Breasts with Hazelnuts and Orange Potato Balls *70*

Quick Turkey à la king *71*

SWEDISH MEATBALLS WITH SOURED CREAM AND DILL SAUCE

The meatball mixture can be made really quickly using a good processor. Serve with casseroled red cabbage or kidney beans and baked potatoes for a colourful meal cooked in the oven.

Serves 6
1½ cups / 225 g / 8 oz lean beef
1½ cups / 225 g / 8 oz lean pork
1½ cups / 225 g / 8 oz veal
1 small onion, peeled and quartered
1 clove garlic, peeled
1 tablespoon parsley
1 tablespoon fresh dill
5 tablespoons double (heavy) cream
1 egg, beaten to mix
salt and cayenne pepper
1 teaspoon Worcestershire sauce
3 tablespoons oil
2 tbsp / 25 g / 1 oz butter
Sauce: 1 tablespoon fresh dill
⅝ cup / 300 ml / ½ pint soured cream
salt and freshly ground pepper
1 tbsp vermouth or Pernod

Set the oven at 350 F / 180 C / Gas 4.

Dice the meats, and chop very finely using the metal blade. Remove and set aside. Using the same blade, finely chop the onion with the garlic and fresh herbs. Keeping the machine running, replace the meat, and gradually add the cream and beaten egg through the feed tube. Finally, add a little salt, cayenne pepper and the Worcestershire sauce.

Fry a teaspoon of the mixture and taste for seasoning. The mixture should not be too bland. Chill for 20 minutes.

Using wet hands, shape the chilled mixture into small balls 2.5 cm / 1 inch in diameter. Heat the oil and butter in a large, shallow flame-proof casserole. Add the meatballs and carefully brown on all sides – you may have to do this in batches. Cook the browned meatballs in the heated oven for about 30 minutes, or until they are cooked right through.

Meanwhile, make the sauce. Finely chop the dill using the metal blade and place in a small pan with the cream. Heat slowly till boiling point, then remove from the heat and leave to infuse for 10 minutes. When the meatballs are cooked, add the vermouth or Pernod to the sauce and season to taste. Pour over the meatballs. Shake the pan gently to mix, then quickly reheat on top of the stove.
Serve immediately.

VITELLO TONNATO

*This summery Italian dish of cold roast veal in a tuna fish
sauce should be made a day or so in advance.
Ask the butcher to bone the veal for you – you will need
the bones for the sauce.*

Serves 6
1 kg / 2 lb piece boned leg or fillet of veal
2 carrots, peeled and halved
2 onions, peeled and halved
2 tbsp / 25 g / 1 oz butter
450 g / 1 lb veal bones
Sauce: 3 egg yolks
1 cup / 200 ml / 7 fl oz olive oil
1 to 2 tbsp lemon juice
1 cup / 184 g / 6½ oz can tuna fish
salt and freshly ground pepper
Garnish: 1 tbsp capers
lemon wedges

Set the oven at 400 F / 200 C / Gas 6.

Trim the veal and tie into a neat cylinder if necessary.
Using the metal blade, coarsely chop the carrots and
onions. Put half the vegetables in a roasting pan and set
the meat on top. Rub with the butter and roast in the
heated oven for 1½ to 1¾ hours, basting frequently.
Remove from the tin and allow to cool completely.

Put the remaining vegetables and the veal bones into a
large saucepan, and add the vegetables and meat juices
from the roasting tin. Barely cover with water and bring
to the boil, skimming frequently. Simmer for 1½ to 2
hours. Strain, discarding the bones and vegetables. Boil
the stock rapidly to reduce to 1¼ cups / 300 ml / ½ pint.
Cool.

In the meantime prepare the sauce. Put the egg yolks
in the processor fitted with the metal blade. With the
machine running, make a thick mayonnaise by adding
the oil slowly through the feed tube. Add 1 tbsp of the
lemon juice. Drain and flake the tuna fish, and gradually
add to the sauce through the feed tube while the machine
is running. Add enough stock to the sauce, again
through the feed tube, to make a sauce of coating consistency. Season to taste, adding more lemon juice if
necessary.

Remove the string from the meat and thinly slice. Put
the sliced veal into a terrine and spoon over the sauce.
Cover and chill overnight for the flavours to blend.

Garnish with the capers and lemon wedges. Serve
with crusty bread, and a crisp salad.

LIVER STROGANOFF

*Serve with buttered noodles and a green salad for a balanced,
nutritious meal.*

Serves 4
450 g / 1 lb calve's or lamb's liver
⅝ cup / 150 ml / ¼ pint milk
1 small onion, peeled and quartered
1¾ cups / 100 g / 4 oz button mushrooms
1 tablespoon snipped chives
4 tbsp / 50 g / 2 oz butter
1 tbsp flour
Approx. 2 cups / 425 g / 15 oz can consommé soup
⅝ cup / 150 ml / ¼ pint soured cream
salt and freshly ground pepper
a little lemon juice

Remove any membranes from the liver, then cut into
thin strips 5 cm / 2 inches long. Cover with the milk and
leave to soak for 15 minutes. Drain well, discarding the
milk and pat dry with paper towels.

Meanwhile, using the metal blade, finely chop the
onion and set aside. Wipe the mushrooms, and chop
roughly with the chives, using the metal blade. Set aside.

Heat the butter in a large heavy frying pan or sauté
pan. Sauté the liver over high heat for a minute to seal
and brown. Drain and remove to a plate, reduce the heat,
add the onions to the pan and cook slowly, stirring
frequently for a couple of minutes to soften. Add the
mushroom mixture and fry over medium heat for 1
minute. Stir in the flour and cook, stirring for 1 minute
until golden. Add the consommé, and bring to the boil,
stirring constantly. Finally, add the cream, and simmer
for a couple of minutes, until the sauce is the consistency
of double (whipping) cream. Season to taste with salt,
pepper and lemon juice. Replace the liver and any meat
juices that have collected on the plate and reheat quickly
without boiling. Serve immediately.

CORNED BEEF STUFFED POTATOES

Children of all ages will love this meal in a potato.

Serves 4 to 6
4 large potatoes, scrubbed
1 tsp oil
1 tsp salt
1 medium onion, peeled
2 cloves garlic, peeled
1 stick celery
½ green pepper, cored and seeded
1⅓ cups / 75 g / 3 oz button mushrooms, wiped
4 tbsp / 50 g / 2 oz butter
¾ lb / 340 g / 12 oz can corned beef
salt and freshly ground pepper
¾ cup / 75 g /3 oz cheddar cheese

Set the oven at 350 F / 180 C / Gas 4.

Rub the potatoes with the oil and salt and bake in the heated oven for about 1½ hours or until tender.

Meanwhile, using the metal blade, finely chop the onion with the garlic, celery, pepper and mushrooms. Heat the butter in a frying pan, add the vegetables and stir-fry over medium heat for about 5 minutes or until slightly softened.

When the potatoes are ready, slice in half and scoop out the insides. Put into the processor fitted with the metal blade. Dice the corned beef and add. Process briefly, or pulse, until well mixed. Stir into the vegetables in the frying pan and reheat. Season to taste.

Heat the grill (broiler). Pile the mixture back into the potato skins. Grate the cheese, using the grating disc, and sprinkle over the potatoes. Grill until golden and bubbling. Serve immediately, piping hot.

STIR-FRIED BEEF WITH BABY CORN AND GREEN PEPPERS

Serve with plainly boiled rice, and vegetable or shrimp chop suey (page 36), Chinese Chicken (page 56) or Fried Pork, (page 57) for a complete Chinese meal.

Serves 4 to 6
450 g / 1 lb piece lean rump steak
1 tbsp cornflour (cornstarch)
3 green peppers, cored, seeded, and halved
1 green chilli, cored, and seeded
1 small onion, peeled and halved
2 cloves garlic
2.5 cm / 1 inch piece root ginger, peeled
4 tbsp oil
½ tsp castor sugar
283 g / 10 oz can baby corn, drained
1 to 2 tbsp soy sauce, to taste
2 tbsp sherry

Cut the meat into wafer-thin slices, either by hand, or by processor, using the slicing blade (it is best to semi-freeze the meat first if using this method). Coat with the cornflour, and set aside.

Using the slicing disc, slice the peppers, chilli, and onion, and set aside. Using the same disc, slice the garlic and ginger, and set aside.

Heat 1 tablespoon of the oil in a wok or large frying pan. Add the sliced peppers, chilli and onion. Stir-fry over high heat for 2 minutes. Drain thoroughly and set aside.

Heat the remaining oil in the wok or pan, add the ginger and garlic and fry for a few seconds. Add the meat and sugar and stir-fry over high heat for 1 minute, add the corn and stir-fry for another minute. Season with the soy sauce and sherry, and stir-fry the whole mixture for 30 seconds. Finally, add the pepper mixture and stir-fry for 1 or 2 minutes to heat through and blend the flavours. Serve immediately.

CHINESE CHICKEN WITH PINEAPPLE AND CASHEW NUTS

Serve with plainly boiled rice and jasmine tea for a quick and tasty Chinese meal.

Serves 4 to 6

450 g / 1 lb chicken breasts, skinned and boned
3 tsp cornflour (cornstarch)
2.5 cm / 1 inch piece fresh root ginger, peeled
2 cloves garlic, peeled
6 spring onions (scallions), trimmed
3 cups / 240 g / 12 oz can pineapple chunks in natural juice
2 tbsp dry sherry
2 tbsp oil
¾ cup / 75 g / 3 oz cashew nuts
salt

Quarter the chicken breasts, and chop roughly using the metal blade. Coat with 1 teaspoon of the cornflour, and set aside.

Using the slicing disc, slice the ginger and garlic and set aside. Slice the spring onions using the same disc, and set aside.

Drain the juice from the pineapple, and measure 1 cup /200 ml / 7 fl oz. Mix with the remaining cornflour and the sherry.

Heat the oil in a wok or large frying pan, and add the sliced ginger and garlic. Stir-fry for a few seconds, then add the chicken. Stir-fry over high heat, making sure the chicken pieces remain separate. When the chicken has become golden brown (after about 2 minutes), add the cashew nuts, and stir-fry for 1 minute. Add the pineapple and the juice mixture. Bring to the boil, stirring constantly, and cook for another minute. Stir in the onions, and add salt to taste. Serve immediately.

FRIED PORK WITH MUSHROOMS AND WATER CHESTNUTS

The pork can be replaced with lean steak, or boneless, skinned chicken breasts, for a change of flavour.

Serves 4 to 6
450 g / 1 lb pork fillet
1 tsp cornflour (cornstarch)
3½ cups / 225 g / 8 oz button mushrooms
225 g /8 oz can water chestnuts, drained
1 small onion, peeled and quartered
2.5 cm / 1 inch piece fresh root ginger, peeled
4 tbsp oil
1 tbsp soy sauce, or to taste
2 tbsp sherry
1 tbsp Hoi Sin sauce, or to taste
Garnish: 1 tbsp sesame seeds

Cut the meat into large cubes. Using the metal blade, roughly chop the meat. Remove from the machine, and coat with the cornflour. Set aside.

Using the same blade, slice the mushrooms and water chestnuts into small finger-nail sized pieces. Set aside.

Using the metal blade, finely chop the onion and ginger and set aside.

Heat half the oil in a wok or large frying pan, and add the onion mixture. Stir-fry for 1 minute, then add the mushroom mixture, and stir-fry for another minute. Add half of the soy sauce, fry for 30 seconds, then remove the vegetables on to a plate.

Wipe out the wok or pan, add the remaining oil and heat. Add the meat, and stir-fry over high heat to separate the pieces and brown evenly. After 2 minutes, add the remaining soya sauce, the sherry, Hoi Sin sauce and all the vegetables. Stir-fry for 2 minutes, then transfer to a serving dish and serve immediately, sprinkled with sesame seeds.

SAUTE OF LAMB WITH CRANBERRIES

*A colourful dish that is excellent served with Fried Cabbage
(page 37), or Nutty Rice Pilau (page 40).*

Serves 4
4 loin lamb chops
4 cups / 450 g / 1 lb onions, peeled and halved
2 medium carrots, peeled
2 tbsp oil
1 cup / 100 g / 4 oz fresh cranberries
2 tbsp port
2 tbsp redcurrant jelly
2 tbsp stock
salt and freshly ground pepper
Garnish: 1 tbsp parsley

Trim the chops, pat dry and set aside.

Using the slicing disc, slice the onions and set aside.
Using the julienne disc, shred the carrots, or slice using
the slicing disc.

Heat the oil in a sauté pan or heavy deep frying pan,
and brown the chops on each side. Drain and remove.
Add the onions and cook slowly over low heat for 10
minutes. Stir in the carrots and cook for a further 5
minutes. Add the cranberries, port, redcurrant jelly and
stock. Bring to the boil, then add the chops. Shake the
pan well, then cover and simmer for 20 minutes, turning
the chops after 10 minutes. Meanwhile, chop the parsley
using the metal blade.

When the chops are tender, taste for seasoning. The
sauce should not be too wet, however if the cranberries are particularly juicy, remove the chops and keep
warm, then boil the liquid rapidly to reduce to a thick
glaze. Spoon over the chops and serve garnished with
the parsley.

SPICED LAMB AND CHEESE MEATLOAF

Serve hot with Ratatouille (page 35 minus the cheese), or cold with relish or chutney and Rainbow Salad (page 47).

Serves 4 to 6
3 cups / 225 g / 8 oz large spinach leaves, washed
5 thin slices / 100 g / 4 oz crustless granary or wholewheat bread
450 g / 1 lb lean lamb, trimmed
2 eggs, beaten to mix
1 medium onion, peeled and quartered
2 cloves garlic, peeled
1 green chilli, cored and seeded
2 tbsp oil
1 tsp ground coriander
½ tsp ground cumin
salt and freshly ground pepper
100 g / 4 oz Gruyère cheese

Set the oven at 375 F / 190 C / Gas 5.

Grease a 1 kg / 2 lb loaf tin (pan), and line the base with a strip of greased greaseproof or waxed paper.

Remove the stalks from the spinach and blanch in boiling salted water for 1 minute. Drain and rinse with cold water. Drain well, pat dry with paper towels, then line the prepared tin with the spinach leaves so they completely cover the sides and base. Save any spinach leaves which are left-over.

Using the metal blade, process the bread to make fine crumbs. Tip into a bowl.

Cut the lamb into cubes then process with the metal blade until finely chopped. With the machine running, add the eggs through the feed tube. Process for a couple of seconds, then add to the crumbs.

Using the metal blade, process the onion with the garlic and chilli until very finely chopped. Heat the oil in a pan, add the onion mixture and fry for 2 minutes. Stir in the spices and fry for 1 minute. Allow to cool, then add to the bowl with a little salt and pepper. Using the metal blade, chop any remaining spinach and add to the bowl. Mix all these ingredients together until smooth and well blended.

Using the slicing disc, slice the cheese.

Pack half the meat mixture into the loaf tin. Cover with the sliced cheese, then with the remaining meat mixture. Press down firmly with the back of the spoon. Cover the tin with foil, then stand the tin in a roasting pan half-filled with hot water. Bake in the heated oven for 1¾ to 2 hours. Turn out and serve sliced.

STUFFED CABBAGE LEAVES

The venison can be replaced with lean beef, pork, or veal. This traditional dish is best served with brown rice, or Jansson's Temptation (page 32), or boiled noodles tossed in butter and black pepper.

Serves 4 to 6
1½ cups / 225 g / 8 oz lean venison, trimmed
⅔ cup / 100 g / 4 oz lean pork, trimmed
100 g / 4 oz fat belly pork
1 tsp salt
1 tsp ground black pepper
¼ tsp ground nutmeg
1 tbsp parsley
1 tsp fresh thyme
12 large cabbage (savoy type)
12 rashers (slices) streaky bacon
1⅞ cups / 450 ml / ¾ pint well-flavoured gravy

Set the oven at 375 F / 190 C / Gas 5.

Grease an oven-proof casserole dish.

Dice the venison and lean and fat pork. Using the metal blade, chop the meat with the seasonings and herbs to the consistency of sausage meat. Fry a little of the mixture and taste for seasoning. Add more salt, pepper and nutmeg as necessary – the mixture should be well seasoned. Roll into 12 balls.

Blanch the cabbage leaves in boiling salted water for 2 minutes. Drain, refresh with cold water and dry well. Cut out the white stalk, then wrap each meatball in a cabbage leaf. Use the back of a knife to stretch the bacon rashers. Wrap a rasher of bacon securely round each cabbage parcel. Place the 12 parcels in the prepared casserole, and pour over the gravy.

Bring to the boil on top of the stove, then cover and cook in the heated oven for 1 hour. Serve piping hot.

CURRY-FRIED TURKEY

Serve hot with Nutty Rice Pilau (page 40), or Spicy Potatoes (page 33), or cold with a tossed green salad, and a rice salad.

Serves 4
675 g / 1½ lbs turkey breasts, boned and skinless
2 cloves garlic, peeled
2.5 cm / 1 inch piece fresh root ginger, peeled
3 medium tomatoes, peeled
1 tsp tomato purée (aste)
½ tbsp fresh coriander leaves
½ tsp ground turmeric
½ tsp salt
1 tsp ground cumin
½ tsp ground fennel
¼ tsp ground nutmeg
¼ tsp ground cinnamon
2 drops Tabasco
2 tbsp oil

Freeze the turkey until very firm. Slice using the slicing disc, then turn into a shallow glass or china bowl. Using the metal blade, process the garlic with the ginger.

Add all the remaining ingredients, except for the oil and process for 20 seconds. Tip into the glass bowl and stir into the sliced turkey until well mixed. Cover and leave to marinate overnight in the fridge.

When ready to serve – heat the oil in a heavy sauté pan or heavy, deep-frying pan. Add the meat and the marinade and fry over medium high heat for about 10 minutes, stirring frequently, until the turkey is golden brown and slightly crispy.

Variation: replace the turkey with lean steak, chicken breasts, fillet of lamb or pork, or pheasant breasts.

PORK DIJONNAISE

Serve noodles tossed in butter and black pepper or creamy mashed potatoes to complement the rich piquant sauce.

Serves 4
4 pork chops
2 shallots, peeled
2 tbsp oil
⅝ cup / 300 ml / ½ pint dry white wine
bouquet garni
salt and freshly ground pepper
2 egg yolks
2 tbsp Dijon mustard
1 tbsp parsley
4 tbsp soured cream

Trim the chops and pat dry. Using the metal blade, finely chop the shallots.

Heat the oil in a heavy sautè or frying pan, and brown the chops on both sides. Stir in the shallots and cook for 1 minute. Add the wine, bouquet garni and a little salt and pepper. Stir well, bring to the boil, then cover and cook very gently for 20 minutes or until the chops are tender.

Using the metal blade, process the yolks with the mustard and parsley. Drain the juices from the meat and skim off the fat, then with the machine running, pour the hot juices on to the egg yolk mixture in the processor through the feed tube. Process for 10 seconds, then pour in the cream. Process briefly. Taste the sauce for seasoning then pour over the chops. Reheat without boiling and serve immediately.

Variation: replace the chops with boneless chicken breasts, or veal chops.

LAMB WITH FENNEL AND LEMON SAUCE

This dish comes from Greece. If you wish, you can replace the lamb with pork, chicken, veal or turkey.

Serves 6
2 bulbs fennel, trimmed
1 kg / 2 lb lean, boneless lamb
2 medium onions, peeled
2 tbsp parsley
2 tbsp oil
1 tbsp flour
⅝ cup / 150 ml / ¼ pint red wine
2½ cups / 600 ml / 1 pint good lamb, veal or chicken stock
bouquet garni
salt and freshly ground pepper
Sauce: 2 eggs
4 tbsp lemon juice

Slice the fennel using the slicing disc. Blanch in boiling, salted water for 5 minutes. Drain, reserving the stock for soup and refresh the fennel with cold water. Drain thoroughly, and set aside.

Meanwhile, cube the meat and pat dry. Set aside. Using the metal blade, finely chop the onions together with the parsley.

Heat the oil in a heavy, flame-proof casserole or pan and quickly brown the meat on all sides – this may have to be done in several batches. Drain well, remove and set aside on a plate.

Add the blanched fennel and the chopped onion and parsley to the casserole and cook over low heat for 10 minutes until soft and golden, stirring occasionally. Stir in the flour, cook for 1 minute, then stir in the wine, half the stock, and the bouquet garni, and bring to the boil, stirring constantly. Replace the meat, add a little salt and pepper, then cover and simmer gently for 1½ hours or until tender, stirring from time to time.

Make the sauce just before serving – process the eggs with the lemon juice for 5 seconds using the metal blade.

Bring the remaining stock to the boil, remove from the heat and leave to cool for 1 minute. Then pour the hot stock into the machine through the feed tube with the machine running. Remove the casserole from the heat, and stir in the sauce. Taste and adjust the seasoning. Cover and leave to stand in a warm place, or on top of a hot plate for 10 minutes, for the flavours to blend. Serve with new potatoes, or plainly boiled rice.

PHEASANT POJARSKI CROUTES

Serve as a first course or light main course, with Mushroom Sauce, (page 66), and a green salad. The pheasant can be replaced with chicken, veal, scallops, or fillet of sole.

Serves 6
1¼ cups / 65 g / 2½ oz crustless white bread, diced
225 g / 8 oz pheasant breasts, boned and skinned
⅝ cup / 150 ml / ¼ pint soured cream
1 tbsp port
¼ tsp salt
2 drops Tabasco
freshly ground black pepper
To serve: 6 slices granary bread, toasted
6 large, flat mushrooms
2 tbsp / 25 g / 1 oz butter
6 sprigs parsley

Set the oven at 400 F / 200 C / Gas 6.

Using the metal blade, process the bread to form fine crumbs. Reserve. Dice the pheasant and process for 10 to 15 seconds using the metal blade, until finely chopped. Add the crumbs, cream, port and seasonings and process for 30 seconds or until very smooth. Fry a teaspoon of the mixture and taste for seasoning – it should not be too bland. Turn into a bowl and allow to chill until firm – about an hour.

Cut the toast into circles 7.5 cm / 3 inches in diameter and place on a baking sheet.

Put the chilled pheasant mixture into a piping bag fitted with a star nozzle, and pipe the mixture neatly on to the croûtes. Bake in the heated oven for 10 to 15 minutes until golden and firm to touch.

While the pojarski are cooking, fry the mushrooms using the butter and drain on kitchen paper.

Serve each croûte piping hot, capped with a mushroom and garnished with a sprig of parsley. Serve with mushroom sauce.

MUSHROOM SAUCE

Serve with Pheasant Pojarski Crôutes (as in previous recipe), chops, escalopes of chicken, turkey or veal, or with pasta.

Serves 4 to 6
1 small onion, peeled
2 tbsp / 25 g / 1 oz butter
1¾ cups / 100 g / 4 oz firm white button mushrooms
2 tbsp / 15 g / ½ oz flour
⅝ cup / 150 ml / ¼ pint chicken stock
⅝ cup / 150 ml / ¼ pint whole milk or light cream
1 tbsp port (optional)
salt and freshly ground pepper
pinch of nutmeg
1 tbsp snipped chives
lemon juice to taste

Using the metal blade, finely chop the onion. Heat the butter in a small pan and slowly cook the onion until soft and golden. Using the slicing disc, slice the mushrooms. Add to the onions and fry over medium heat for 2 minutes. Stir in the flour and cook for 1 minute. Stir in the stock and milk or cream and bring to the boil, stirring constantly. Add the port, and seasonings. Simmer the sauce for 5 minutes. Chop the chives using the metal blade and stir into the sauce and add a little lemon juice to taste.

CHICKEN STUFFED WITH FRUIT AND NUTS

A lovely, moist stuffing, full of flavour. Serve with brown rice and Fried Cabbage (page 37).

Serves 6
1 1.5 kg / 3½ lb oven ready chicken
2 medium onions, peeled
2 slices / 50 g / 2 oz crustless granary bread
¼ cup / 25 g / 1 oz roasted almonds
¼ cup / 25 g / 1 oz roasted hazelnuts
½ cup / 100 g / 4 oz butter
1 large cooking apple, peeled and cored
½ cup / 75 g / 3 oz apricots
½ cup / 75 g / 3 oz prunes, stoned
2 tbsp / 25 g / 1 oz pine nuts
1 tbsp raisins
salt and freshly ground pepper
1 tbsp fresh thyme
⅝ cup / 300 ml / ½ pint good chicken stock

Set the oven at 400 F / 200 C / Gas 6.

Wipe the chicken inside and out and season inside. Quarter one of the onions and place in a roasting pan. Dice the bread and process with the metal blade, to form fine crumbs. Set aside. Using the same blade, roughly chop the almonds and hazelnuts. Set aside. Finely chop the other onion with the same blade. Heat half the butter in a frying pan and slowly cook the onion until soft and golden.

In the meantime, chop the apple, apricots and prunes to small finger-nail size using the metal blade. Add to the onion and fry for 1 minute. Then add the chopped almonds, hazelnuts, pine nuts and raisins to the pan. Take the pan off the heat and mix in the breadcrumbs. Add a tablespoon of the stock and season with salt and pepper. Cool, then use to stuff the chicken. Stand the chicken on the onion in the roasting pan. Rub with the remaining butter, sprinkle with salt and pepper and the thyme. Roast in the heated oven for about 1¼ hours, basting frequently.

Remove the cooked chicken to a warmed serving dish, and keep warm. Add the stock to the pan, and bring to the boil on top of the stove, stirring to dislodge all the meat juices. Skim off any fat. Boil the gravy till reduced by a third. Season to taste, then strain and serve.

HOT GAME PIE WITH FRIED APPLES AND ONIONS

Wild Duck is particularly good cooked this way, although any sort of game can be used. Try to mix at least two types of game for the best flavour.

Serves 4 to 6
Pastry: 225 g / 8 oz plain wholemeal flour
large pinch salt
2 tbsp / 25 g / 1 oz lard or white vegetable fat
6 tbsp / 75 g / 3 oz butter or hard margarine
1 egg
1 to 2 tbsp milk
Filling: 240 g / 1 lb cooked game, boned
⅔ cup / 100 g / 4 oz streaky bacon
6 tart apples, quartered and cored
2 large onions, peeled
4 tbsp / 50 g / 2 oz butter
1 tsp castor sugar
salt and freshly ground pepper
mild paprika to taste
½ cup / 150 - 200 ml / 5 - 7 fl oz left-over game gravy
Glaze: 1 egg, beaten to mix

Set the oven at 400 F / 200 C / Gas 6.

Make the pastry first. Put the flour and salt in the processor fitted with the metal blade. Roughly dice the fats and add. Process until the mixture resembles fine crumbs. Mix the egg with 1 tablespoon of the milk and add to the mixture through the feed tube with the machine running. The mixture should form a soft but not sticky dough. If too dry add a little more milk. Wrap and chill while preparing the filling.

Cut or shred the game into bite-sized chunks, and reserve. Using the metal blade, coarsely chop the bacon. Set aside. Fit the slicing disc, and slice the unpeeled apples. Set aside. Using the same disc, slice the onions and set aside from the apples.

Heat half the butter in a frying pan, and fry the bacon till golden brown and crispy. Drain and remove. Fry the onions till soft and golden. Drain and remove. Heat the remaining butter and quickly fry the apple slices with the sugar till caramelized. Drain and remove.

Layer up the filling in a greased pie dish (pie plate) in this order – onions, bacon, apples, game, onion, apple, game, apple, onions and finally bacon. Add seasoning with each layer. Pour over enough of the gravy to come ⅔ the way up the dish.

Roll out the pastry on a floured board to an oval 5 cm / 2 inches larger than the dish. Cut a strip the width of the rim of the dish. Brush the rim with a little of the beaten egg. Stick the pastry strip on to the rim then brush with egg. Cover the pie dish with the pastry. Seal well and flute the edges. Cut a small steam-hole in the top. Decorate the pie with any trimmings of pastry if wished. Glaze with beaten egg.

Bake in the heated oven for 10 minutes, then reduce the heat to 375 F / 190 C / Gas 5, and bake for a further 20 minutes or until the pastry is crisp and golden brown. Serve hot.

DUCK BREASTS WITH HAZELNUTS AND ORANGE POTATO BALLS

The potato mixture can be made in advance, then fried just before serving. Duck breasts are now available from many supermarkets.

Serves 4 to 6
Potato Balls:
6 cups / 1 kg / 2 lb potatoes, peeled
2 oranges
4 tbsp / 50 g / 2 oz butter
3 egg yolks
3 small eggs
salt and freshly ground pepper
1 cup / 100 g / 4 oz hazelnuts
2 tbsp flour
oil for deep-frying
Duck and sauce:
2 large duck breasts, boned
2 tbsp oil
½ cup / 50 g / 2 oz hazelnuts
½ small onion
1 tsp flour
⅝ cup / 150 ml / ¼ pint duck or chicken stock
1 large orange
1 tsp chunky marmalade
salt and freshly ground pepper

First make the potato mixture. Halve the potatoes and cook in boiling salted water until tender. Drain well, then return to the pan and dry over low heat for 1 minute. Grate the rind from the oranges and set aside. Use the juice extractor or citrus juicer to extract the juice from the oranges. Set aside. Put the potatoes into the processor fitted with the metal blade. Add the orange rind and juice, the egg yolks, and 2 of the eggs. Add salt and pepper to taste. Process very briefly until smooth. Spoon on to a plate, cover and chill until firm.

Roll tablespoonfuls of the potato mixture into balls. Using the metal blade, finely chop the nuts. Roll the potato balls in seasoned flour, then in the remaining egg, beaten, and finally roll in the nuts. Chill for 15 minutes or until ready to serve.

Heat the oil to 180 C / 350 F and fry the balls a few at a time till golden brown. Remove from pan, i.e. drain on paper towels and keep warm.

To cook the duck – trim the breasts if necessary. Heat the oil in a frying pan and fry the duck for about 3 minutes on each side for rare meat, longer for medium and well done meat. Drain and keep warm. Fry the hazelnuts in the fat in the pan for a couple of minutes or until browned. Drain and remove. Finely chop the onion using the metal blade, and add to the pan. Fry for a couple of minutes to soften then add the flour. Fry for 1 minute stirring constantly, then stir in the stock. Bring to the boil, stirring, then simmer for 2 minutes.

Grate the orange rind and set aside, extract the juice as above, then stir the rind and juice into the sauce with the marmalade. Bring to the boil and season to taste. Thinly slice the duck, adding any juices to the sauce. Arrange the duck slices on a warmed serving dish with the potatoes. Stir the fried hazel nuts into the sauce and spoon over the meat. Serve immediately.

QUICK TURKEY A LA KING

The turkey can be replaced with chicken, pheasant or veal. Serve with buttered noodles, boiled rice or toast fingers.

Serves 4
450 g / 1 lb cooked turkey, boned and skinned
1¾ cups / 100 g / 4 oz white button mushrooms
1 small green pepper
1 small red pepper
2 tbsp / 25 g / 1 oz butter
6 tbsp dry sherry
1¼ cups / 300 ml / ½ pint soured cream
salt and freshly ground pepper
2 egg yolks

Cut the turkey into large cubes. Process or pulse briefly to chop coarsely. Reserve. Wipe and trim the mushrooms. Peel the peppers by grilling (broiling) until the skin becomes charred and wrinkled. Wrap in a damp tea-towel then place in a plastic bag, and leave for 5 minutes. Unwrap the peppers and peel off the charred skin with a small knife. Remove the core and seeds from the peppers and quarter. Using the metal blade, process the peppers and mushrooms and chop until the size of peas.

Heat the butter in a frying pan and fry the pepper/ mushroom mixture over medium heat for 2 to 3 minutes or until softened. Add half of the sherry and bring to the boil. Stir in the cream, a little salt and pepper, and simmer gently for a couple of minutes, then add the turkey and simmer for a further 2 minutes.

Process the yolks with the remaining sherry using the metal blade. With the machine running, pour in a little of the hot sauce (strained to remove the vegetables) through the feed tube, process for a couple of seconds. Pour the yolk mixture into the frying pan and stir well. Reheat without boiling. Taste for seasoning and serve immediately.

FISH AND SHELLFISH

Kipper Roulade *74*

Hot Haddock Mousse *75*

Cod Provençal *76/77*

Trout with Avocado and Ham *78*

Salmon and Chive Cocottes *79*

Haddock with Vegetables and Cream *80*

Salmon and Sole Turban *81*

Mackerel with Spiced Walnut Stuffing *82*

Two Trout Mousse *83*

Goujons with 'Hot' Tomato Sauce *84*

Seafood Rissoles *85*

Monkfish in Whisky Sauce with Spinach Timbales *86*

Shrimp Toasties *87*

Fish and Vegetable Timbales *88/89*

Seafood Salad *90*

Smoked Fish Salad *91*

Fish Risotto with Apricots *92*

Prawn (Shrimp), Pineapple and Coconut Curry *93*

KIPPER ROULADE

This is really a rolled-up soufflé, filled with tomatoes and cucumbers. If you wish, serve with Mushroom Sauce (page 66).

Serves 4 to 6

175 g / 6 oz kipper fillets, cooked
3 eggs, separated
1 tbsp snipped chives
1 tbsp parsley
3 tsp lemon juice
4 tbsp / 50 g / 2 oz butter or margarine
½ cup / 50 g / 2 oz flour
¾ cup / 175 ml / 6 fl oz whole milk
freshly ground black pepper
Filling: 3 medium tomatoes, skinned and quartered
10 cm / 4 inch piece cucumber, peeled and quartered
freshly ground black pepper
1 tsp lemon juice

Set the oven at 200 C / 400 F / Gas 6.

Grease a Swiss roll tin (jelly-roll pan). Line with greased bakewell paper, making sure the sides stand 1 cm / ½ inch high. Secure the corners with paper clips.

Skin the fish, then put into the processor bowl fitted with the metal blade. Add the egg yolks, chives, parsley and lemon juice. Process for 5 seconds, till just mixed.

Melt the butter in a small pan, stir in the flour, then the milk. Bring to the boil, stirring constantly, to make a thick sauce. Pour in the fish mixture in the processor and process for 5 seconds, or until well-mixed and smooth. Season to taste with black pepper. Transfer to a bowl.

Stiffly whisk the egg whites, either using the whisk attachment or by hand, and carefully fold into the fish mixture. Spoon into the prepared case and bake in the heated oven for 10 to 12 minutes till just firm to the touch.

Make the filling while the roulade is cooking. Using the metal blade, process the tomatoes and the cucumber with a little black pepper and the lemon juice till roughly chopped. Place in a strainer to drain off the juices. Leave to dry.

Turn out the roulade on to a piece of bakewell paper, spread with the filling and roll up, using the bakewell paper to help you. Don't worry if the roulade starts to crack. Serve immediately.

HOT HADDOCK MOUSSE

This can be prepared in advance and reheated when ready to eat. Serve with a Hollandaise Sauce (page 81).

Serves 4 to 6
2 cups / 100 g / 4 oz crustless white bread, cubed
350 g /12 oz cooked, smoked haddock, boned and skinned
1 tbsp lemon juice
1 hard-boiled egg, peeled and quartered
1 tbsp parsley
1 stick celery, roughly chopped
½ green pepper, cored, seeded and quartered
1½ tbsp / 20 g / ¾ oz butter
3 tbsp / 20 g / ¾ oz flour
⅝ cup / 250 ml / 8 fl oz milk
150 ml / ¼ pint single (light) cream
1 egg, beaten to mix
salt and freshly ground pepper
Set the oven at 350 F / 180 C / Gas 4.

Grease and line a 500 g / 1 lb loaf tin (pan).

Using the metal blade, process the bread to make fine crumbs. Add the fish, lemon juice, hard-boiled egg, parsley, celery and the green pepper to the processor. Process for 10 seconds.

Melt the butter in a small pan. Stir in the flour, then the milk and cream. Bring to the boil, stirring constantly. Simmer for 1 minute, cool slightly, and add to the fish mixture in the processor bowl with the beaten egg. Process briefly to mix all the ingredients. Season to taste. Spoon into the prepared tin and bake in the heated oven for 30 minutes. Turn out and serve, with new potatoes and salad.

COD PROVENCAL

*A really simple, colourful dish. If you wish, serve on a bed of
rice. You can use any white fish
steaks, or tuna fish, though this needs cooking longer.*

Serves 4
4 × 175 g / 6 oz cod steaks
2 tbsp lemon juice
3 tbsp flour
salt and freshly ground pepper
3 tbsp olive oil
1 small onion, peeled
2 cloves garlic, peeled
3 large, ripe tomatoes, peeled and seeded
1 teaspoon tomato purée (paste)
1 anchovy fillet
2 tbsp / 25 g / 1 oz butter
Garnish: ½ cup / 75 g / 3 oz black olives, stoned

Wash the fish and pat dry. Sprinkle with lemon juice,
and leave to marinate for about 2 hours.

Season the flour with a little salt and pepper, and coat
the fish. Heat the olive oil in a sauté pan or deep frying
pan. Fry the fish for about 4 minutes on each side, till
golden brown and firm. Drain, remove and keep warm.

Using the metal blade, finely chop the onion with the
garlic, tomatoes, tomato purée and anchovy fillet. Add to
the oil in the pan, and cook for 5 to 10 minutes till thick
and pulpy, stirring frequently. Remove from the heat
and taste for seasoning. Stir in the butter, and spoon over
the fish. Garnish with the olives and serve.

TROUT WITH AVOCADO AND HAM

These days trout are so easily available that traditional ways of cooking them can seem a little plain. This unusual filling will transform them.

Serves 4
4 × 225 g / 8 oz trout, cleaned
4 tbsp lemon juice
1 large ripe avocado pear
½ cup / 75 g / 3 oz sliced lean ham
salt and freshly ground pepper
8 thin rashers (slices) streaky bacon
2 tbsp flour
6 tbsp / 75 g / 3 oz butter
Garnish: lemon wedges

Sprinkle the trout inside and out with half the lemon juice and a little salt.

Peel the avocado and remove the stone. Process the flesh with the remaining lemon juice until smooth, using the metal blade. Add the ham, and process until the ham is finely chopped but not puréed. Season to taste. Spoon this stuffing into the fish cavities.

Stretch the bacon rashers with the back of a knife, and wrap two rashers securely round each fish. Dust the fish with the flour. Heat the butter in a large frying pan, and fry the fish for 4 to 5 minutes on each side, till the flesh is opaque and the skin is browned. Serve at once with lemon wedges.

SALMON AND CHIVE COCOTTES

Serve as a light lunch or as a first course, hot or cold.

Serves 4
175 g / 6 oz cooked salmon, boned
½ cup / 50 g / 2 oz cheddar cheese
3 eggs
2 egg yolks
1¼ cups / 300 ml / ½ pint single (light) cream
1 tbsp snipped chives
salt and freshly ground pepper
Set the oven at 375 F / 190 C / Gas 5.

Butter 4 small individual dishes.

Skin and flake the salmon and divide among the dishes.

Using the grating disc, grate the cheese. Fit the metal blade, and process the cheese with the remaining ingredients. Pour over the salmon in the dishes. Place in a roasting pan half-filled with hot water. Bring to the boil on top of the stove, then bake in the heated oven for 15 minutes or until firm to the touch. Serve at once, or leave to cool.

HADDOCK WITH VEGETABLES AND CREAM

The haddock can be replaced with any other white fish fillets — plaice, sole, whiting, halibut, turbot, cod, monkfish, bluefish, scrod.

Serves 4 to 6
800 g / 1½ lb haddock fillets, skinned
2 large carrots, peeled
2 medium leeks, trimmed, halved and washed
1 small onion, peeled and halved
6 tbsp / 75 g / 3 oz butter
1¼ cup / 300 ml / ½ pint double (heavy) cream
salt and freshly ground pepper
1 tbsp snipped chives
1 tbsp vermouth

Wash and dry the fish. Cut into large cubes and reserve. Shred the carrots, leeks and onions using the julienne or grating disc. Melt 4 tbsp / 50 g / 2 oz of the butter in a sauté pan or deep frying pan. Add the vegetables and stir-fry for 1 minute over high heat. Add the fish, cream and a little seasoning. Shake the pan gently to mix the ingredients. Carefully pack the fish over low heat for 5 minutes, shaking the pan from time to time. Remove from the heat, and gently stir in the chives, remaining butter and the vermouth. Taste for seasoning, and serve immediately with new potatoes and courgettes (zucchini).

Haddock with vegetables and cream

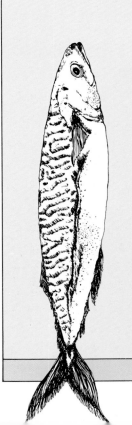

SALMON AND SOLE TURBAN

A very elegant dinner party dish. The centre can be filled attractively with a prawn (shrimp) sauce, or watercress.

Serves 6

450 g / 1 lb fish fillets, skinned – salmon, sole, whiting or haddock, or a mixture
⅝ cup / 150 ml / ¼ pint double (heavy) cream
salt and freshly ground pepper
¼ tsp horseradish cream
3 egg whites

The turban:

400 g / 14 oz sole fillets, skinned
400 g / 14 oz salmon escalopes

Prawn (Shrimp) hollandaise sauce:

1 cup / 225 g / 8 oz unsalted butter
4 egg yolks
1 tbsp lemon juice
1 tbsp hot water
salt and freshly ground pepper
¾ cup / 100 g / 4 oz frozen prawns (shrimps), thawed and warmed
Garnish: 1 bunch watercress

Set the oven at 350 F / 180 C / Gas 4.

Butter a 4 cup capacity / 1 litre / 1½ pint ring mould.

First make the filling. Dice the fish fillets, and using the metal blade, process with the cream, a little salt and pepper and the horseradish to a smooth purée. Transfer to a bowl set over ice. Stiffly beat half the egg whites, using the whisk attachment, or by hand, and beat into the fish mixture. Poach a little of the mixture in boiling water to taste for seasoning. Add more salt, pepper and horseradish if necessary. Cover and chill the fish mixture for a minimum of 2 hours, and a maximum of 6 hours. Stiffly beat the remaining egg whites, as above, and fold into the chilled mixture.

For the turban – put the fillets between 2 sheets of clingfilm (plastic wrap) and very gently flatten out using a food mallet, rolling pin or base of a small pan. Cut each fillet in half diagonally. Cut the salmon escalopes into strips the same size. Use the sole fillets and salmon strips to line the mould, alternating the white and pink strips, with the 'skinned' side of the fish on the inside. Leave the ends of the fish hanging over the edges of the mould. Spoon in the filling, then fold the ends of the fish in on top. Cover with buttered aluminium foil and stand the mould in a roasting tin (pan) half-filled with hot water. Bring to the boil on top of the stove, then cook in the heated oven for 30 to 40 minutes or until firm. Turn out on to a warmed serving plate.

To make the sauce – bring the butter to the boil. Process the yolks with the lemon juice, hot water and seasoning, using the metal blade. With the machine running, slowly pour in the hot butter through the feed tube. Taste for seasoning. Remove the lid and stir in the warmed prawns with a spatula. Tip into a warmed serving bowl. Garnish the turban with watercress in the centre, if you wish. Serve immediately.

MACKEREL WITH SPICED WALNUT STUFFING

An European version of a traditional Middle Eastern dish.

Serves 4
4 mackerel, cleaned
salt and freshly ground pepper
Stuffing: 2 large onions, peeled and halved
2 tbsp olive oil
1 cup / 100 g / 4 oz shelled walnuts
½ tbsp of fresh coriander
¼ tbsp ground cumin
¼ tsp ground cinnamon
pinch ground nutmeg
½ tsp turmeric
3 limes
Set the oven at 375 F / 190 C / Gas 5.

Grease 4 large pieces of aluminium foil.

Rinse the fish and pat dry. Season inside and out. Set each fish in the middle of a piece of foil.

To prepare the stuffing: slice the onions using the slicing disc. Heat the oil in a frying pan, and slowly cook the onions till soft and golden brown. Meanwhile, use the metal blade to coarsely chop the walnuts and coriander. Stir into the cooked onions with the spices and season to taste. Fry for 1 minute. Divide the stuffing into 4 parts, and spoon a portion into the cavity of each fish.

Use the slicing disc to slice one of the limes. Arrange the slices on top of the mackerel. Squeeze the remaining limes to extract the juice, using the citrus juicer or juice extractor, or by hand. Pour the juice over the fish, and securely wrap each fish in its sheet of foil. Place on a baking sheet and bake in the heated oven for 30 to 40 minutes, till the flesh is opaque, and the fish cooked through to the bone. Serve hot or cold with garlic bread and a tossed green salad.

FISH
AND SHELLFISH

TWO TROUT MOUSSE

An unusual combination of fresh and smoked trout.

Serves 4 to 6
1½ tbsp / 20 g / ¾ oz butter
3 tbsp / 20 g / ¾ oz flour
⅝ cup / 300 ml / ½ pint milk
2 egg yolks
2 tsp horseradish cream
salt and freshly ground pepper
⅝ cup / 150 ml / ¼ pint sunflower or safflower oil
1 tsp wine vinegar
⅝ cup / 150 ml / ¼ pint double (heavy) cream
¼ lb / 100 g / 4 oz smoked trout
¼ lb / 100 g / 4 oz cold, poached trout, boned
2 sticks celery
lemon juice to taste
½ large cucumber, peeled

Melt the butter in a small pan, stir in the flour, followed by the milk. Bring to the boil, stirring constantly until sauce is smooth and creamy. Simmer for 1 minute, then leave to cool completely.

Put the yolks into the processor fitted with the metal blade, and process for 5 seconds with the horseradish cream and a little salt and pepper. With the machine running, slowly pour in the oil through the feed tube to make a thick mayonnaise. When all the oil has been added, mix in the vinegar. Add the cooled sauce and process for 10 seconds till well mixed. Turn into a mixing bowl. Stiffly whisk the cream using the whisk attachment or the plastic blade, and add to the mayonnaise mixture.

Flake both types of trout, discarding the skin. Using the metal blade, finely chop the celery. Carefully fold into the mayonnaise mixture with the fish. Add lemon juice and season to taste. Using the slicing disc, slice the cucumber. Pat the slices dry on paper towels. Use half the slices to line the base and sides of a 17.5 to 20 cm / 7 to 8 inch glass soufflé dish. Spoon in half the fish mixture. Cover with a layer of cucumber slices, then the remaining fish mixture. Decorate with the remaining cucumber slices. Cover and chill for at least 2 hours. Serve with slices of toast or buttered pumperknickel, and a green salad.

GOUJONS WITH 'HOT' TOMATO SAUCE

Another dinner party dish, this time a first course of crispy fillets of fish served with a piquant sauce of tomatoes and chillis.

Serves 4 to 6
675 g / 1½ lb cod or sole fillets, skinned
8 thin slices / 175 g / 6 oz crustless white bread
½ cup / 50 g / 2 oz flour
salt and freshly ground pepper
2 eggs, beaten to mix
oil for deep-frying
Sauce:
2 medium onions, peeled and halved
2 cloves garlic, peeled
2 tbsp / 25 g / 1 oz butter
1 red chilli, cored and seeded
2 green chillis, cored and seeded
2.5 cm / 1 inch piece fresh root ginger, peeled
5 medium tomatoes, peeled and seeded
3 tsp tomato purée (paste)
1 tbsp brown sugar
1 tbsp vinegar
2 tbsp water
salt

Rinse and dry the fish, cut into thin slices diagonally. Using the metal blade, process the bread to form fine crumbs. Season the flour with a little salt and pepper and use to coat the fish. Dip in beaten egg and roll in the crumbs. Shake off the excess, and chill the fish. In the meantime prepare the sauce.

Using the slicing disc, slice the onions with the garlic. Heat the butter in a frying pan, and fry the onion mixture till golden brown. Using the metal blade, finely chop the chillis, ginger and tomatoes. Add the remaining ingredients and process for a couple of seconds to mix. Add to the onions in the frying pan. Cook, stirring frequently, over medium heat until the sauce is very thick. Taste the sauce, it should be very piquant. Add more salt, sugar, or vinegar as necessary. Spoon into a serving bowl and keep warm.

Heat the oil to 180 C / 355 F and fry the fish in batches till golden brown and crispy. Drain on kitchen paper. Sprinkle with a little salt if wished and served immediately with the hot sauce.

Goujans with hot tomato sauce

SEAFOOD RISSOLES

Serve as a first course with a tossed green salad, or Hot Tomato sauce (page 84).

Makes 12
Pastry:
3 cups / 300 g / 11 oz plain flour
¼ tsp salt
⅝ cup / 150 g / 5 oz unsalted butter
2 egg yolks
approx. 4 tbsp milk to mix
1 beaten egg to seal
Filling:
1 small onion, peeled
1 tbsp parsley
2 tbsp / 25 g / 1 oz butter
¾ cup / 100 g / 4 oz frozen prawns (shrimps), thawed
¾ cup / 150 g / 5 oz cooked, shelled crabmeat
1½ cups / 175 g / 6 oz cooked scallops
1 hard-boiled egg, peeled and quartered
salt and freshly ground pepper
2 tsp Mayonnaise (see page 42)
oil for deep-frying

First make the pastry. Using the metal blade, process the flour with the salt. Dice the butter, and process with the flour until the mixture resembles fine crumbs. Mix the egg yolks with the milk and add to the mixture through the feed tube with the machine running. Process until a soft but not sticky dough is formed, adding more milk if necessary. Wrap and chill while preparing the filling.

For the filling: finely chop the onion with the parsley and soften in the butter over low heat for 2 minutes. Using the metal blade, coarsely chop the prawns with the crab, scallops and egg. Season to taste. Stir in the onion mixture and mayonnaise.

Roll out the pastry 3 mm / ⅛th inch thick and cut out 12 rounds, each 10 cm / 4 inches in diameter. Put a little filling in the centre of each round. Brush the edges of the pastry with beaten egg, then fold the pastry over to form semi-circles. Seal the edges well. Chill for 30 minutes.

Heat the oil to 180 C / 355 F and fry the rissoles a few at a time for 5 minutes till golden brown. Drain well on kitchen paper and serve with Hot Tomato Sauce.

MONKFISH IN WHISKY SAUCE WITH SPINACH TIMBALES

A very easy but impressive fish dish. (If Monkfish is not available use sole or other white fish.) Serve with tiny new potatoes and carrots.

Serves 6
Timbales:
6 cups / 450 g / 1 lb washed fresh spinach, stalks removed
3 tbsp cream cheese
salt and freshly ground pepper
4 eggs, beaten to mix
Fish:
675 g / 1½ lb monkfish or white fish fillets
1 small onion, peeled and halved
½ cup / 100 g / 4 oz unsalted butter
4 tbsp whisky
2 tbsp lemon juice
salt and freshly ground pepper
Set the oven at 350 F / 180 C / Gas 4.

Grease 6 individual moulds or deep dishes.

First prepare the timbales – dry the spinach well and tear up the leaves. Process, using the metal blade with the remaining ingredients given for the timbales, till finely chopped but not puréed. Pour into the prepared moulds, then stand the moulds in a roasting pan half-filled with hot water. Bring to the boil on top of the stove, then cook in the heated oven for 15 to 20 minutes or until a cocktail stick inserted into the centre of the mixture comes out clean.

Meanwhile cook the fish – remove any skin or membranes from the fish, then wash and pat dry. Cut into scallops approx. 1 cm / ½ inch thick and 5 cm / 2 inches in size. Finely chop the onion using the metal blade.

Heat half the butter in a sauté or frying pan. Fry the onion till soft and golden. Raise the heat and fry the fish for a couple of minutes on each side. Warm the whisky in a small pan and flame. Pour the lemon juice and whisky on to the fish. Shake the pan well, then season to taste. Remove the pan from the heat and add the remaining butter cut into small pieces. Stir gently to mix.

Turn out the timbales on to a warmed serving plate, and spoon the fish into the centre. Serve immediately.

SHRIMP TOASTIES

*This makes an excellent snack meal served with a
crisp green salad.*

Serves 4
4 thick slices bread
2 tbsp / 25 g / 1 oz soft butter
2 cups / 225 g / 8 oz gruyere cheese
salt and freshly ground pepper
1 tbsp flour
2 eggs
¾ cup / 100 g / 4 oz frozen shrimps, thawed
1 tbsp snipped chives
2 tomatoes

Butter the bread on one side only. Place buttered side
down on a baking sheet.

Using the grating disc, grate the cheese. Empty out,
and fit the processor with the metal blade. Process the
cheese with a little salt and pepper, the flour and one of
the eggs. When the mixture is smooth, add the remaining egg. Process for 30 seconds. Tip into a bowl and chill
the mixture until it is spreadable.

Meanwhile, coarsely chop the prawns with the chives,
using the metal blade. Set the oven to the highest temperature. Stir the prawns into the cheese mixture. Slice
the tomatoes, and arrange on top of the bread. Spread
thickly with the prawn mixture and bake in the heated
oven for 5 minutes or until brown and bubbling.
Serve immediately.

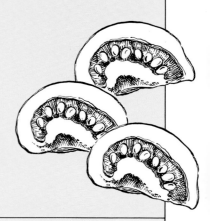

FISH AND VEGETABLE TIMBALES

Use sole, haddock, turbot or scallops for the creamy fish mixture. These timbales are delicious served with a Hollandaise Sauce (page 81), minus the prawns (shrimps).

Serves 6
Fish mixture:
450 g / 1 lb white fish fillets, skinned
1 tbsp lemon juice
4 eggs, beaten to mix
1⅞ cups / 450 ml / ¾ pint double (heavy) cream
1 tbsp snipped parsley, chives or chervil or a mixture
salt and freshly ground pepper
2 medium carrots
⅔ cup / 50 g / 2 oz French beans, blanched
Garnish: 1½ cups / 350 g / 12 oz long grain rice
1 medium carrot, peeled
⅔ cup / 50 g / 2 oz French beans
1 tbsp parsley
2 tbsp / 25 g / 1 oz butter
salt and freshly ground pepper
Set the oven at 325 F / 160 C / Gas 3.

Butter 6 large individual moulds or large, deep dishes.

Cut the fish into cubes and process with the lemon juice, using the metal blade, until very smooth. With the machine running, gradually add the eggs through the feed tube, followed by the cream and chives. Season to taste. Cover and chill until ready to assemble.

Using a channelling knife, flute one of carrots. Then slice the rest of it using the slicing blade. Blanch in boiling salted water for 2 minutes. Drain and refresh with cold water. Press on to the base and sides of each of the moulds to form an attractive design. Using the julienne disc, shred the remaining carrot. Cook in boiling salted water until just tender. Drain and refresh. Top and tail the beans and cut into pieces 1 cm / ½ inch long. Blanch in boiling salted water until just tender. Drain and refresh.

Put a little fish mixture into each mould and smooth the surface. Cover with a layer of beans, then another layer of fish followed by a layer of carrots, then fish again, then the remaining beans, and finally a layer of fish. Cover the moulds with buttered foil, then stand in a roasting pan half-filled with hot water. Bring to the boil on top of the stove, then cook in the heated oven for 20 minutes.

Meanwhile, prepare the garnish – cook the rice in boiling salted water until tender. Drain and rinse with boiling water. Drain well. While the rice is cooking, shred the carrots using the julienne disc and cook in boiling salted water until just tender. Top and tail the beans and cut into 1 cm / ½ inch lengths. Cook as for the carrots. Drain the vegetables. Chop the parsley, using the metal blade. Stir into the rice with the vegetables, butter, and seasonings. Cover and keep warm in the oven till ready to serve.

To serve: spoon the rice on to a warmed serving plate, turn out the timbales and arrange on top of the rice. Serve with the Hollandaise Sauce (page 81) spooned over or served separately.

SEAFOOD SALAD

Serve as a first course or as a light lunch with thinly sliced brown bread watercress sandwiches.

Serves 4 to 6
100 g / 4 oz smoked salmon
¾ cup / 100 g / 4 oz frozen prawns (shrimps), thawed
½ lb / 225 g / 8 oz cold, cooked monkfish, white fish or salmon
1¼ cups / 300 ml / ½ pint Avocado Mayonnaise (page 42)
Tabasco sauce
lemon juice
1 hard green apple, quartered and cored
3 sticks celery, quartered
1 small green pepper, cored, seeded and halved

Using the metal blade, coarsely chop the smoked salmon. Turn into a bowl and mix with the prawns, flaked fish, and the mayonnaise. Season to taste with Tabasco sauce and lemon juice.

Using the metal blade, coarsely chop the apple. Stir into the mayonnaise. Using the slicing disc, slice the celery and pepper. Stir into the mayonnaise. Serve immediately.

SMOKED FISH SALAD

A lovely, light summer-time salad.

Serves 4
350 g / 12 oz smoked mackerel fillets, skinned
1½ cups / 225 g / 8 oz pasta bows
1¼ cups / 300 ml / ½ pint Yogurt Mayonnaise (page 42)
1 tsp curry paste
1 tsp tomato purée (paste)
salt and freshly ground pepper
1¾ cups / 100 g / 4 oz firm white button mushrooms
1 medium courgette (zucchini)
2 sticks celery
Garnish: cherry tomatoes
½ crisp lettuce

Flake the fish and put into a mixing bowl. Cook the pasta in boiling salted water until just tender. Drain and refresh with cold water. Dry thoroughly, then add to the fish.

Using the metal blade or plastic blade, mix the mayonnaise with the curry paste and the tomato purée. Season to taste. Add to the fish and pasta. Wipe the mushrooms, courgette and celery, and slice using the slicing disc. Mix into the other ingredients and adjust the seasoning. Arrange on a bed of lettuce leaves, garnished with cherry tomatoes. Serve with garlic bread.

Smoked fish salad

FISH RISOTTO WITH APRICOTS

This fruity risotto makes an interesting change from paella.

Serves 6
1 large onion, peeled and quartered
4 tbsp / 50 g / 2 oz butter
2 cups / 450 g / 1 lb brown rice, washed
3¾ cups / approx 900 ml / 1½ pints fish stock or water
bouquet garni
½ cup / 75 g / 3 oz apricots
¾ cup /75 g / 3 oz toasted almonds
⅔ cup / 75 g / 3 oz large, seedless raisins
½ lb / 225 g / 8 oz monkfish or other white fish fillets, skinned
¾ cup / 100 g / 4 oz frozen prawns (shrimps), thawed
¾ cup / 100 g / 4 oz cooked mussels, shelled
salt and freshly ground pepper

Using the metal blade, finely chop the onion. Heat the butter in a sauté pan or paella dish. Add the onion and cook slowly for 3 minutes. Add the rice and fry for 1 minute. Stir in the stock and bouquet garni. Bring to a boil and simmer very gently for 20 minutes.

Using the metal blade, coarsely chop the unsoaked apricots and almonds. Stir into the rice with the raisins. Cut the fish into strips and stir in. If the rice is a bit dry, add a little more stock to prevent the mixture from sticking to the pan. Simmer for 10 minutes, then stir in prawns and mussels. Taste for seasoning. Simmer for 5 more minutes, or until the rice is cooked and the liquid has been absorbed. Season to taste.

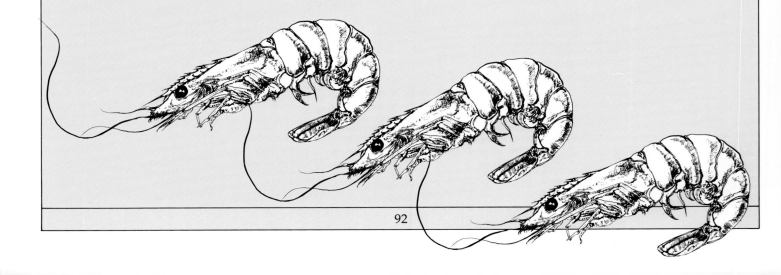

PRAWN (SHRIMP), PINEAPPLE AND COCONUT CURRY

An Indonesian recipe which is ideal for serving with rice or Spicy Potatoes (page 33).

Serves 4
½ cup / 100 g / 4 oz creamed coconut
1 large onion, peeled and quartered
2 cloves garlic, peeled
1 green chilli, seeded and cored
2 tbsp oil
1 clove
3 green cardamons
1 cinnamon stick
2 tsp ground coriander
½ tsp ground cumin
pinch nutmeg
pinch cayenne pepper
salt
1 large, ripe pineapple, peeled
3 cups / 450 g / 1 lb frozen prawns (shrimps), thawed

Using the metal blade, process the creamed coconut with 1¼ cups / 300 ml / ½ pint boiling water, and tip into a jug. Leave to stand as directed on the packet. Using the metal blade, finely chop the onion with the garlic and chilli. Heat the oil in a sauté pan or wok, and stir-fry the onion mixture with the whole spices for 2 minutes until golden. Add the ground spices and a little salt. Stir-fry for a moment. Quarter the pineapple and remove the core, then coarsely chop using the metal blade. Add to the wok or pan with the creamed coconut. Stir well, then simmer for 3 minutes. Stir in the prawns and simmer for a further 2 minutes. Taste for seasoning and serve.

PUDDINGS AND DESSERTS

Frinton Fruit Tart 96

Date, Lemon and Walnut Sponge Pudding 97

Fruit Pancakes 98

Healthy Rhubarb Crumble 99

Chocolate Macaroon Pud 100

Apples Stewed in Wine 101

Mango and Lime Sorbet 102

Quick Apple and Orange Tart 103

Steamed Apple and Lemon Pudding 104

Gingered Pear Crunch 105

Hazelnut Gâteau 106

Blackberry and Apple Ice-Cream 108

Lime Tart 109

Ritzy Pudding 110

Rhubarb and Ginger Cheesecake 111

Velvet Mousse 112

Frozen Apricot Dessert 112

FRINTON FRUIT TART

A lovely end to a meal. Serve warm or cold with cream or ice-cream.

Serves 6 to 8

Pastry:

3 cups / 300 g / 11 oz plain flour
¼ cup / 25 g / 1 oz ground almonds
1 tbsp / 25 g / 1 oz sugar
6 tbsp / 75 g / 3 oz lard or white vegetable fat
6 tbsp / 75 g / 3 oz butter or margarine
6 tbsp milk

Filling:

⅓ cup / oz walnut halves
⅓ cup / 40 g / 1½ oz hazelnuts
¼ cup / 40 g / 1½ oz flaked almonds
2 tbsp / 25 g / 1 oz glacé cherries
2 tbsp / 25 g / 1 oz currants
2 tbsp / 25 g / 1 oz sultanas
½ cup / 75 g / 3 oz raisins
2 tbsp / 25 g / 1 oz long shred desiccated coconut
2 tbsp / 25 g / 1 oz soft brown sugar
1 egg, beaten to mix
2 tbsp / 25 g / 1 oz butter, melted
icing sugar to dust

Set the oven at 375 F / 190 C / Gas 5.

Make the pastry first. Using the metal blade, process the flour with the ground almonds and sugar for seconds. Dice the fats, and add to the flour. Process for 15 to 20 seconds until the mixture resembles fine crumbs. With the machine running, pour in the milk to make a soft but not sticky dough. Wrap and chill till firm.

When the pastry is ready, make the filling. Using the metal blade, coarsely chop the walnuts with the hazelnuts. Tip into a mixing bowl. Stir in the almonds. Using the metal blade, roughly chop the cherries. Add to the bowl of nuts with the currants, sultanas, raisins and coconut. Process the sugar with the egg and melted butter, using the metal blade, for 20 seconds. Stir into the dry ingredients and mix well.

Roll out the pastry 3 mm / ⅛th inch thick. Use half the pastry to line a deep 22.5 cm to 25 cm / 9 to 10 inch pie plate. Spread over the filling. Cover with the remaining pastry. Seal the edges well and flute. Make a steam-hole in the top, and use the remaining pastry trimmings to decorate.

Bake in the heated oven for about 25 minutes until the pastry is golden brown. Heat the grill. Dust the pie with icing sugar and very, very briefly grill (broil) until the sugar caramelizes and forms a shiny glaze. This has to be done carefully, turning the pie constantly to avoid burning.

DATE, LEMON AND WALNUT SPONGE PUDDING

If you like steamed puddings, you'll adore this one.

Serves 4
Topping:
1 tablespoon lemon curd
Pudding:
1 cup / 100 g / 4 oz self-raising flour (if not available use plain flour and 1 extra tsp of baking powder)
large pinch baking powder
6 tbsp / 75 g / 3 oz butter
3 tbsp / 75 g / 3 oz castor sugar
2 tbsp lemon curd
2 eggs
⅓ cup / 50 g / 2 oz stoned dates
½ cup / 50 g / 2 oz walnut halves
Sauce:
⅝ cup / 150 ml / ¼ pint double (heavy) cream
3 tbsp lemon curd

Butter a 4 cup capacity / 900 ml / 1½ pint pudding basin (baking dish).

Spread the lemon curd topping evenly over the base of the basin.

Using the metal blade, process the flour, with the baking powder, butter and sugar for 10 seconds. Beat the lemon curd with the eggs and add to the processor. Process for 20 seconds or until well-mixed and creamy. Stop the machine and add the dates and nuts. Pulse 4 to 5 times to mix well and coarsely chop the dates and nuts. Spoon into the basin. Cover loosely with greased aluminium foil, tying it firmly with string around the rim to prevent water from getting in. Stand the basin in a pan of simmering water, so the water comes ⅔ the way up the bowl. Cover and steam for 1½ hours, topping up the water, as needed, to prevent the pan boiling dry.

Turn the pudding out on to a serving plate, and serve piping hot with the sauce.

For the sauce: using the whisking attachment or plastic blade, half-whisk the cream. Add the lemon curd and whisk again until the cream is thick and light. Spoon into a bowl for serving.

Date, Lemon and walnut pudding

FRUIT PANCAKES

An unusual version of the traditional pancake from Germany. It is delicious served with ice-cream.

Serves 4
Batter:
1 cup / 100 g / 4 oz plain flour
1 egg
1 egg yolk
1¼ cups / 300 ml / ½ pint milk
1 tsp vegetable oil
1 tsp castor sugar
Filling:
2 eating apples, peeled, cored, quartered and sliced
1 tbsp sultanas
1 tbsp castor sugar
½ tsp mixed spice
To fry:
a little vegetable oil

Make the batter first – process the flour with the egg and yolk and a little of the milk. With the machine running, add the remaining milk. Process till smooth. With the machine running, add the oil and sugar. Leave the batter to stand for 30 minutes.

Slice the apples using the slicing disc. Heat a very little oil in a non-stick frying pan. Add a little of the batter and tilt the pan to evenly coat the base. Cook for a few seconds to set. Cover with a few apple slices and a few of the sultanas. Pour over a little more batter, then using a spatula, flip the pancake over. Cook till browned on each side. Fold in half and tip out of the pan. Sprinkle with a little sugar and mixed spice. Repeat with remaining batter and fruit. Serve hot.

HEALTHY RHUBARB CRUMBLE

The rhubarb can be replaced with apples, apricots, or pears.

Serves 6
675 g / 1½ lb young rhubarb
1 orange
⅓ cup / 75 g / 3 oz soft brown sugar, or to taste
Topping:
2 cups / 175 g / 6 oz rolled oats
1 tbsp wheatgerm
1 tbsp sesame seeds
1 cup / 100 g / 4 oz mixed nuts – cashews, walnuts, almonds, hazelnuts
½ tsp ground cinnamon
⅓ cup / 75 g / 3 oz dark, soft brown sugar
1 tbsp raisins
6 tbsp / 75 g / 3 oz butter or margarine
Set the oven at 350 F / 180 C / Gas 4.

Wash the rhubarb and cut into 1 cm / ½ inch lengths.

Grate the rind from the orange, and extract the juice using the citrus juicer or the juice extractor. Mix with the rhubarb and the brown sugar. Put into an oven-proof baking dish.

For the topping, mix the oats with the wheatgerm, and sesame seeds. Using the metal blade, chop the nuts as finely or as coarsely as you wish. Mix into the oats with the cinnamon, sugar and raisins. Heat the butter in a frying pan, and fry the topping mixture for 2 minutes, stirring constantly. Cool, then spoon over the rhubarb. Bake in the heated oven for 30 to 40 minutes or until the fruit is tender. Serve warm or cold with yogurt.

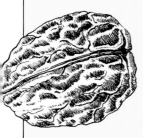

CHOCOLATE MACAROON PUD

This heavenly mixture of rich chocolate and almondy macaroons is delicious served with coffee cream.

Serves 4
1 cup / 175 g / 6 oz stale macaroons
1 cup / 100 g / 4 oz dark chocolate
1 tbsp water
1 cup / 225 g / 8 oz butter
225 g / 8 oz castor sugar
4 eggs, separated
½ cup / 50 g / 2 oz flour
To serve:
⅝ cup / 150 ml / ¼ pint double (heavy) cream
castor sugar to taste
1 tbsp powdered (not granules) coffee

Set the oven at 350 F / 180 C / Gas 4.

Grease a 17.5 cm / 9 inch soufflé dish.

Use the metal blade to chop half the macaroons into coarse crumbs. Set aside. Use the same blade to make the remaining macaroons into fine crumbs. Set aside.

Grate the chocolate using the grating disc. Put into a bowl set over a pan of hot, but not boiling, water. Add the water and gently melt. Remove from the heat and leave aside to cool.

Use the metal blade to cream the butter with the sugar and yolks. With the machine running, gradually add the flour and the fine crumbs, followed by the chocolate. Spoon into a mixing bowl. Stiffly whisk the egg whites using the whisking attachment and fold in with the coarse crumbs. Spoon into the soufflé case and bake for 40 minutes till firm to the touch.

In the meantime, make the coffee cream. Using the whisking attachment, whisk the cream with the coffee and sugar till thick. Chill.

The pudding can be served hot, warm or cold.

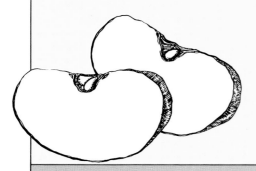

APPLES STEWED IN WINE

A lovely autumn dish, best made with tart cooking apples and a crisp, dry white wine.

Serves 4

6 medium cooking apples, peeled, cored and quartered
4 tbsp / 50 g / 2 oz butter
⅝ cup / 150 ml / ¼ pint white wine
⅝ cup / 150 ml / ¼ pint water
¾ cup / 175 g / 6 oz castor sugar
grated rind and juice of 1 lemon
a cinnamon stick
1 clove
½ cup / 75 g / 3 oz stoned Muscat raisins

Slice the apples using the slicing disc.

Heat the butter in a large pan and fry the apples till golden, about 3 minutes. Put the remaining ingredients into a pan and heat slowly to dissolve the sugar. Bring to the boil and simmer for 5 minutes. Carefully pour over the apples. Simmer for a few minutes until the apples are tender. Remove the cinnamon stick and the clove and serve warm with custard, yogurt or cream.

MANGO AND LIME SORBET

This is a favourite Mexican recipe with a fresh, tangy flavour.

Serves 6
2½ cups / 600 ml / 1 pint water
225 g / ½ lb castor sugar
2 limes
3 large, ripe mangoes, peeled and stoned
2 egg whites

Put the sugar and water into a pan and heat gently to dissolve the sugar. Bring to the boil, and simmer for 5 minutes. Remove from the heat and cool completely. Grate the rind from the limes and extract the juice using the citrus juicer, or by hand. Purée the mangoes with the lime rind and juice using the metal blade. With the machine running, gradually pour in the sugar syrup. Pour into a freezing container. Cover and freeze till the mixture becomes slushy.

Stiffly whisk the egg whites using the whisking attachment, turn into a bowl and reserve. Using the metal blade, process the half-frozen mango and lime sorbet for a few seconds till smooth and foamy. Tip into the bowl of egg whites and carefully fold in. Freeze until firm. Soften slightly, then spoon into the processor bowl. Process with the metal blade till smooth. Re-freeze overnight, and serve within a week.

QUICK APPLE AND ORANGE TART

A different version of a classic French recipe.

Serves 4 to 6

2 cups / 225 g / 8 oz Rough Puff Pastry (page 27) or frozen puff pastry, thawed
6 tbsp orange marmalade
1 tsp lemon juice
4 tart eating apples
sliced glacé cherries (optional)

Set the oven at 400 F / 200 C / Gas 6.

Grease a baking sheet.

Roll out the pastry very thinly, and use to completely cover the baking sheet, trimming off any excess (this will depend on the size of your baking sheet). Prick well, then chill for 30 minutes.

Heat the marmalade with the lemon juice and beat until smooth, then set aside. Halve and core the apples but don't peel. Slice using the slicing disc. Brush the pastry with a thin layer of marmalade. Cover completely with a neat, even layer of apple slices and a few slices of glacé cherries to add colour. Brush with a little marmalade. Bake in the heated oven for 15 minutes till golden. Heat the remaining marmalade, and brush over the hot tart. Serve hot or warm.

STEAMED APPLE AND LEMON PUDDING

This is guaranteed to keep out the chills of winter.

Serves 6
1 tbsp golden syrup
5 slices / 100 g / 4 oz crustless white bread
1 medium cooking apple, peeled and cored
1¼ cups / 150 g / 5 oz flour
1 level tsp baking powder
½ cup / 100 g / 4 oz suet
½ cup / 100 g / 4 oz castor sugar
grated rind and juice of 1 lemon

Grease a 5 cup capacity / 1 litre / 2 pint pudding basin. Spoon the syrup into the base of the bowl.

Using the metal blade, process the bread to form fine crumbs. Tip into a bowl. Quarter the apple, and grate using the grating disc. Weigh out 1 cup / 100 g / 4 oz of the grated apple. Using the plastic blade, combine the crumbs with the flour, baking powder, suet, grated apple, sugar and the lemon rind and juice. Mix to a soft dough. Transfer to the pudding basin (baking dish). Cover loosely with a piece of greased aluminium foil, and tie securely around the rim with string. Place in a pan of simmering water, so the water comes ⅔ of the way up the basin. Cover and simmer gently for 2 hours, making sure the pan doesn't boil dry.

Turn out and serve with custard or cream.

GINGERED PEAR CRUNCH

If you fancy a change from sherry trifle try this instead.

Serves 4
225 g / 8 oz ginger biscuits
300 ml / ½ pint double (heavy) cream
1 tbsp Marsala
2 tbsp sugar
2 medium-sized pears, peeled
2 pieces stem ginger, drained

Use the metal blade to just break up the ginger biscuits, a few at a time. Set aside. Using the whisking attachment, or plastic blade, half-whisk the cream. Gradually whisk in the Marsala and sugar till the cream is thick. Set aside.

Core and quarter the pears and slice using the slicing disc. Set aside. Finely chop the ginger using the metal blade. Gently fold the ginger and pears into the cream. Layer the gingernuts and cream mixture in individual glasses or an attractive bowl. Chill for ½ to 1 hour.

HAZELNUT GATEAU

Sheer luxury! The same filling can be used to layer up thin meringue rounds.

Serves 8
Gateau:
¾ cup / 175 g / 6 oz softened butter
¾ cup / 175 g / 6 oz castor sugar
1½ cups / 175 g / 6 oz self-raising flour
1 tsp baking powder
3 eggs, beaten
1 tsp coffee essence
Filling:
2 cups / 225 g 8 oz hazelnuts, blanched
1¼ cups /300 ml / ½ pint double (heavy) cream
¼ cup / 50 g / 2 oz sugar
coffee essence to taste
Decoration:
a few whole hazelnuts
Set the oven at 350 F / 180 C / Gas 4.

Grease and line 2 × 17.5 cm / 7 inch sandwich cake tins (pans). Using the metal blade, process the butter with the sugar, flour, and baking powder for 5 seconds. Beat the eggs with the essence and add to the bowl. Process for 20 seconds, till smooth. Divide between the tins, and smooth flat. Bake in the heated oven for 20 to 25 minutes till firm to the touch, and golden. Turn out on to a wire rack and leave to cool. Split each cake in half horizontally.

Roast the hazelnuts in the oven till a good golden brown colour. Cool, then grind coarsely using the metal blade. Set aside. Using the whisking attachment or the plastic blade, stiffly whip the cream, in batches. Stir in the nuts and sugar using a spatula.

Use half the cream to sandwich the layers of the cake together. Flavour the remaining cream with a little coffee essence, and spread over the top and sides of the cake. Decorate with a few whole hazelnuts. Keep chilled until ready to serve

BLACKBERRY AND APPLE ICE-CREAM

Although this tastes best made with blackberries and apples from your garden, frozen blackberries are excellent.

Serves 6 to 8
3 cups / 450 g / 1 lb blackberries
2 large cooking apples, peeled and cored
3¾ cups / 900 ml / 1½ pints double cream
1 cup / 225 g / 8 oz castor sugar
7 eggs, separated

Rinse the blackberries and put into a pan. Quarter and slice the apples, using the slicing disc. Cook slowly with the blackberries to a thick pulp. Purée using the metal blade, then sieve to remove the seeds. Cool.

Using the whisking attachment, or plastic blade, whisk the cream with 1 tablespoon of the sugar till thick (you may have to do this in several batches). Turn into a mixing bowl. Whisk the egg whites to a stiff peak using the whisking attachment. Gradually whisk in all but 2 tablespoons of the remaining sugar. Pile on top of the cream in the mixing bowl. Whisk the egg yolks with the remaining sugar till thick, using the whisking attachment. Stir the yolk mixture into the cream and egg white with the purée. Spoon into a freezing container. Cover and freeze till firm. Serve within a week. This recipe doesn't need whisking or stirring during freezing.

LIME TART

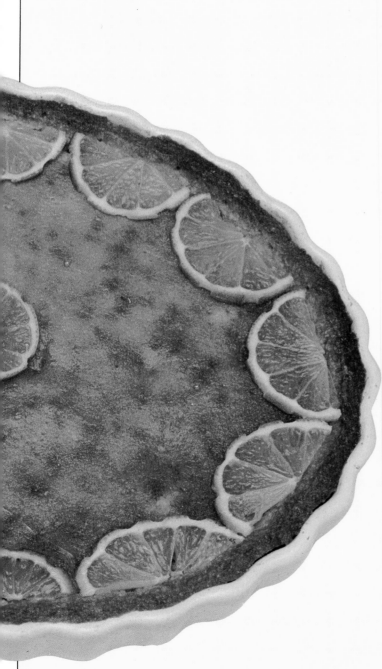

This recipe is said to come from Florida, where it is served with chocolate sauce.

Serves 6
Pastry:
2¼ cups / 225 g / 8 oz flour
2 tbsp / 25 g / 1 oz almonds, blanched
¼ cup / 50 g / 2 oz castor sugar
½ cup / 100 g / 4 oz butter
1 whole egg, beaten
Filling:
2 large eggs
½ cup / 90 g / 3½ oz castor sugar
2 limes
⅓ cup / 90 g / 3½ oz unsalted butter, melted
50 g / 2 oz ground almonds
Set the oven at 375 F / 190 C / Gas 5.

Using the metal blade, process the flour with the almonds till smooth and fine. Add the sugar and process for a couple of seconds. Cut up the butter and add. Process until the mixture resembles fine crumbs. With the machine running, gradually pour in the beaten egg through the feed tube. Mix to a soft but not sticky dough. Wrap and chill till firm. Roll out the pastry 3 mm / ⅛th inch thick and use to line an 20 cm / 8 inch flan tin. Prick well, and bake blind in the heated oven for 10 to 12 minutes. Cool. Reduce the oven to 350 F / 180 C / Gas 4.

Using the whisking attachment, whisk the eggs with the sugar till very thick and light. Grate the lime rind and stir in. Extract the juice from the limes using the citrus juicer or by hand, and stir in using the plastic blade. Using the same blade, mix the melted butter into the lime filling with the almonds. Pour into the pie shell, and bake in the heated oven for 20 to 25 minutes till golden and firm. Cool, then chill overnight.

RITZY PUDDING

It sounds most peculiar, but tastes divine!

Serves 4 to 6

100 g / 4 oz plain Ritz crackers
¼ cup / 25 g / 1 oz candied peel
½ cup / 50 g / 2 oz walnuts
½ cup / 50 g / 2 oz toasted hazelnuts
1 cup / 225 g / 8 oz vanilla sugar
½ tsp baking powder
⅓ cup / 50 g / 2 oz raisins
3 egg whites
topping:
1 cup / 250 ml / 8 fl oz thick, Greek-style yogurt
fresh fruit – strawberries, cherries, raspberries, peaches, bananas, kiwis, apples

Set the oven at 325 F / 160 C / Gas 3.

Grease an 20 cm / 8 inch sandwich tin. Line the base with greased greaseproof paper.

Using the metal blade, process the crackers till they form fine crumbs. Tip into a bowl. Finely chop the nuts and the peel in the same way. Add to the crumbs with the sugar, baking powder and raisins.

Stiffly beat the egg whites using the whisking attachment and fold into the dry ingredients. Spoon into the tin and bake in the heated oven for about 30 minutes till crisp and dry. Cool then turn out.

Spread with the yogurt, and decorate with the fresh fruit. Serve immediately.

RHUBARB AND GINGER CHEESECAKE

A lovely combination of tart fruit, fragrant ginger and a soft, creamy texture.

Serves 8
Base:
12 ginger biscuits
4 tbsp / 50 g / 2 oz butter, melted
Topping:
450 g / 1 lb young rhubarb
2.5 cm / 1 inch piece fresh root ginger, peeled
½ cup / 100 g / 4 oz soft light brown sugar
3 eggs, beaten
1 cup / 175 g / 6 oz cream cheese
1 tsp powdered gelatine
1 tbsp water
⅝ cup / 150 ml / ¼ pint double (heavy) cream

Using the metal blade, process the biscuits to form fine crumbs. With the machine running, pour in the butter through the feed tube. Mix well, then press the base mixture into a 20 cm / 8 inch oiled springform tin. Chill in refrigerator till firm.

Wash and trim the rhubarb. Cut into short lengths, and slice, using the slicing disc. Grate the ginger using the grating disc. Then fit the metal blade, and process the ginger with the sugar to make a fine ginger-sugar. Put into a pan with the fruit and cook till soft and pulpy. Cool slightly, then process with the eggs for 10 seconds. Return to the pan, reheat and cook gently until the mixture thickens. Stir constantly. Leave to cool completely.

Using the metal blade, process the cheese until smooth. Add the rhubarb mixture and process till very smooth. Sprinkle the gelatine over the water and leave to soak for 1 minute, then dissolve. Pour into the processor with the machine running to mix into the cheese-rhubarb mixture. Tip into a bowl. Using the whisking attachment, or plastic blade, whisk the cream till thick and light. Carefully fold into the rhubarb mixture using a spatula. Spoon on to the base and chill till firm. Unmould before serving. Cream, ginger or grated chocolate can be used as decoration

VELVET MOUSSE

Serves 6
1½ cups / 175 g / 6 oz dark chocolate
5 tbsp very strong freshly made black coffee
1 tbsp / 25 g / 1 oz castor sugar
3 eggs, separated
1¼ cups / 300 ml / ½ pint double (heavy) cream

Using the grating disc, grate the chocolate. Leave the chocolate in the processor bowl. Heat the coffee with the sugar and stir until dissolved. Change to the metal blade and with the machine running, pour the coffee in through the feed tube on to the chocolate. Process until smooth. Add the egg yolks and process for 10 seconds. Tip into a bowl. Using the whisking attachment, stiffly whisk the egg whites and fold into the chocolate mixture in stages. Using the whisking attachment or plastic blade, beat the cream to soft peak stage, and fold into the chocolate mixture.

Spoon into individual glasses, chill till firm and decorate with grated chocolate, if you wish.

FROZEN APRICOT DESSERT

A refreshing summertime treat.

Serves 4
2 × 411 g / 14½ oz cans apricots in apple juice
250 ml / 8 fl oz thick, Greek-style yogurt
a little sugar to taste

Drain the apricots, reserve the juice for a fruit salad. Using the metal blade, process the fruit briefly, till coarsely chopped. Pour into a freezer container. Stir in the yogurt and a little sugar to taste. Cover and freeze till firm. Break up into pieces and process with the metal blade till smooth and foamy. Pour back into the container, cover, and freeze overnight until firm.

CAKES,
BISCUITS AND SCONES

Chocolate Mousse Cake *116*

Tina's Coffee-Time Cake *118*

Cheese Shortbreads *119*

Easy Fruit Cake *120*

Hazelnut Shorties *121*

Chocolate Crunch *121*

Coffee Walnut Cake *122*

Fruity Flapjack *123*

Brownies *124*

Cream Buns *125*

Muesli Scones *126*

CHOCOLATE MOUSSE CAKE

A moist rich cake, filled with a fluffy mousse instead of the usual buttercream.

Cake mixture:
1½ cups / 175 g / 6 oz self-raising flour*
2 tbsp cocoa powder
1 tbsp powdered drinking chocolate
½ cup / 100 g / 4 oz golden syrup
½ cup / 100 g / 4 oz castor sugar
½ cup / 100 g / 4 oz butter
⅝ cup / 150 ml / 5 fl oz milk
1 egg
1 tbsp rum
Filling:
1 cup / 100 g / 4 oz dark chocolate
3 tbsp / 15 g / 1½ oz butter
3 eggs, separated
½ tbsp rum
Decoration:
chocolate leaves or curls, or grated chocolate

*Where self raising is not available use plain flour and 1 tsp baking powder.

Set the oven at 350 F / 180 C / Gas 4.

Grease and line 2 × 19 cm / 7½ inch sandwich cake tins (pans).

Using the metal blade, process the flour with the cocoa and drinking chocolate. Melt the syrup with the sugar and butter, and beat the milk with the egg. With the machine running, pour the melted mixture on to the flour mixture followed by the milk mixture. Process for 10 seconds till well-mixed and smooth. Pour into the prepared tins and bake in the heated oven for 25 to 30 minutes. Turn out on to a wire rack to cool. Split each cake in half horizontally and sprinkle with the rum.

While the cake is in the oven, make the filling. Using the grating disc, grate the chocolate. Put into a china or other oven-proof bowl, and set over a pan of hot but not boiling water, add the butter and melt. Remove from the heat and stir in the yolks and rum. Stiffly whisk the egg whites using the whisking attachment. Carefully fold into the chocolate mixture. Chill till firm, then use to sandwich the cake and cover the top. Decorate with the chocolate leaves or curls, or sprinkle with grated chocolate. Serve within 24 hours.

TINA'S COFFEE-TIME CAKE

A lovely moist cake to serve with mid-morning coffee.

½ cup / 25 g / 4½ oz soft butter
1 cup / 225 g / 8 oz soft brown sugar
2½ cups / 250 g / 8¾ oz plain flour
2 tsp bicarbonate of soda
pinch salt
2 eggs
1 cup / 250 ml / 8 fl oz soured cream
3 cups / 50 g / 2 oz seedless raisins
Filling:
1 cup / 100 g / 4 oz walnut halves
½ cup / 100 g / 4 oz soft dark brown sugar
½ tsp cinnamon

Set the oven at 350 F / 180 C / Gas 4.

Grease and base line a 500 g / 1 lb loaf tin (pan).

Using the metal blade, process the butter and sugar till smooth and creamy. Sift the flour with the bicarbonate and the salt. Mix the eggs with the cream. Add the flour mixture and the egg mixture to the processor bowl. Briefly process or pulse till well mixed. Stop the machine and stir in the raisins using a spatula.

Make the filling by putting all the ingredients into the empty processor bowl, fitted with the metal blade. Pulse or process for a couple of seconds to coarsely chop the nuts. Spoon half the cake mixture into the tin, cover with half the filling, then spoon in the remaining cake mixture. Sprinkle with the rest of the filling. Bake for 35 to 40 minutes, till a skewer inserted comes out clean. Cool in the tin.

CHEESE SHORTBREADS

Serve at tea-time or with drinks, or even with dips or cheese.

Makes 30 to 40
1½ cups / 175 g / 6 oz Parmesan cheese or dry, strong Cheddar
2½ cups / 250 g / 9 oz plain flour
200 g / 7 oz butter, diced
¼ tsp mustard powder
¼ tsp ground pepper
beaten egg to glaze

Set the oven at 400 F / 200 C / Gas 6.

Grease several baking sheets.

Using the grating disc, grate the cheese. Fit the metal blade, and process the cheese with the flour, butter and seasonings till the mixture forms a stiff dough. Turn out on to a floured board and roll out 5 mm / ¼ inch thick and cut into fingers 7.5 cm / 3 inches long and 1 cm / ½ inch wide. Or cut into circles 5 cm / 2 inches in diameter. Place on baking sheets, and prick well. Chill for 20 minutes then brush with the egg and bake in the heated oven for 10 minutes till crisp and golden. Cool on a wire rack.

EASY FRUIT CAKE

This can be kept for a week to mature, and eaten plain, decorated with glacé fruits, or covered with marzipan and iced for a simple Christmas or celebration cake.

3½ cups / 350 g / 12 oz self-raising flour*
1 tsp ground mixed spice
1 cup / 225 g / 8 oz butter, diced
¾ cup / 175 g / 6 oz dark, soft brown sugar
3 eggs, beaten
1 heaped tbsp chunky marmalade
2⅔ cups / 675 g / 1½ lb mixed dried fruit
6 tbsp orange juice

Where self raising flour is not available use plain flour and 1½ tsp of baking powder.
Set the oven at 350 F / 180 C / Gas 4.

Grease and line a 20 cm / 8 inch deep cake tin (pan).

Put the flour and mixed spice into the processor fitted with the metal blade. Process for a couple of seconds to mix. Add the butter, sugar, eggs and marmalade, and process till well mixed. Transfer to a mixing bowl and stir in the dried fruit and the orange juice. Spoon into the tin and bake for 1 hour, then reduce the heat to 300 F / 150 C / Gas 2 and bake for a further 2 hours or until a skewerstick inserted in the centre comes out clean. Cool in the tin, then wrap and keep for a week before cutting.

HAZELNUT SHORTIES

These hazelnut shortbread fingers have a light sandy texture, and a rich, nutty flavour.
This is one recipe that demands butter – margarine is just not the same.

Makes 8 to 10
2¼ cups / 225 g / 8 oz plain flour
3 tbsp / 25 g / 1 oz cornflour (cornstarch)
¾ cup / 175 g / 6 oz butter
⅓ cup / 75 g / 3 oz castor sugar
75 g / 3 oz whole skinned hazelnuts
Set the oven at 325 F / 160 C / Gas 3.

Grease a baking sheet.

Sieve the flours together and put into the processor bowl fitted with the metal blade. Dice the butter and add with the sugar. Process for 15 to 20 seconds, or until the mixture comes together to form a stiff shortbread dough. Wrap and chill for 15 minutes.

Meanwhile, toast the nuts in the heated oven for 5 to 10 minutes or until golden brown. Chop very coarsely, then turn out and leave to cool completely.

Knead the nuts into the shortbread on a floured board then roll out 1 cm / ½ inch thick. Cut into fingers 7.5 cm / 3 inches long and 2.5 cm / 1 inch wide, and place on the prepared baking sheet. Prick well with a fork and bake in the heated oven for 20 to 25 minutes or until the fingers are a very light golden colour and firm. Cool slightly on the sheet then transfer to a wire cooling rack.

CHOCOLATE CRUNCH

Serves 8 to 10
2 cups / 225 g / 8 oz dark chocolate
¾ cup / 175 g / 6 oz butter
2 eggs
¼ cup / 50 g / 2 oz castor sugar
225 g / 8 oz Rich Tea biscuits (plain unsweetened cookies)
½ cup / 50 g / 2 oz ginger biscuits
½ cup / 50 g / 2 oz mixed nuts (walnuts, pecans, brazils, hazelnuts, unsalted peanuts, cashews)
1 tbsp seedless Muscat raisins
1 tbsp sherry (optional)

Oil a Swiss roll tin (jelly-roll pan). Use the grating disc to grate the chocolate. Fit the metal blade, and leave the grated chocolate in the processor bowl. Melt the butter till it boils. With the machine running, slowly pour the hot butter into the processor through the feed tube. Process until the chocolate has melted and is very smooth. Spoon out into a bowl. Using the whisking attachment, whisk the egg with the sugar until very thick and light, then gradually whisk in the chocolate mixture.

Tip out into a large mixing bowl. Break up the biscuits and chop very coarsely using the metal blade. Add to the ingredients in the mixing bowl. Coarsely chop the nuts using the same blade and stir into the chocolate mixture with the remaining ingredients. When well mixed, spoon into the prepared tin and smooth the top. Chill until firm then cut into fingers. Serve from the fridge.

COFFEE WALNUT CAKE

Not for the calorie-conscious, but a real treat.

Cake mixture:
¾ cup / 75 g / 3 oz walnut halves
2¼ cups / 225 g / 8 oz self-raising flour*
1 tsp baking powder
2 level tsp instant coffee powder – not granules
2 tbsp hot milk
¾ cup / 175 g / 6 oz butter, diced
¾ cup / 175 g / 6 oz castor sugar
3 eggs, beaten
Fudge topping:
3 tbsp single (light) cream
1 tsp instant coffee powder, not granules
4 tbsp / 50 g / 2 oz butter
1⅔ cups / 225 g / 8 oz sieved icing sugar
½ cup / 50 g / 2 oz walnut halves to decorate

Set the oven at 325 / 160 C / Gas 3.

Grease and line a 17.5 cm / 7 inch deep cake tin (pan).

Using the metal blade, process the walnuts to chop finely, but not to a powder. Set aside.

Put the flour and baking powder into the processor bowl fitted with the metal blade, and pulse or process for a couple of seconds to mix. Dissolve the coffee in the hot milk, leave to cool, then add to the processor with the butter and sugar. Process briefly then add the eggs and process till smooth and light.

Stop the machine and fold in the nuts with a spatula. Spoon into the tin and bake in the heated oven for about 1½ hours or until a skewer comes out clean. Turn out of the tin and leave to cool.

In the meantime, make the topping. Heat the cream till boiling. Put the coffee, butter and sugar into the processor fitted with the metal blade. Pour in the hot cream and process for 10 to 15 seconds till well mixed.

Turn out into a bowl and chill. When firm, beat with a wooden spoon for a few seconds, then spread on to the cake. Decorate with the walnuts.

FRUITY FLAPJACK

This is a lovely, unusual flapjack, full of fruit and nuts.

Makes 14
1 tbsp / 15 g / ½ oz hazelnuts
1 tbsp / 15 g / ½ oz cashew nuts
1 tbsp / 15 g / ½ oz unsalted peanuts
1 tbsp dates, stoned
2 tbsp / 25 g / 1 oz glacé cherries
1 tbsp / 15 g / ½ oz sesame seeds
100 g / 4 oz butter or margarine
4 tbsp golden syrup
1 tbsp soft dark brown sugar
2⅔ cups / 225 g / 8 oz rolled oats

Set the oven at 350 F / 180 C / Gas 4.

Grease a 18 cm / 7 inch square cake pan.

Using the metal blade, coarsely chop the nuts, depending on how crunchy you wish the flapjack to be.

Spread the nuts on a baking sheet and toast in the heated oven till golden brown, stirring from time to time so the nuts brown evenly. Remove and leave to cool. Using the metal blade, coarsely chop the dates and cherries.

Put the butter, syrup and sugar into a medium-sized frying pan, and melt over low heat. Remove the pan from the heat and stir in all the other ingredients. Press the mixture into the prepared pan and bake in the heated oven for 20 to 25 minutes. Remove, and cut the flapjack into 14 fingers. Leave to cool in the pan.

BROWNIES

Makes 10
1 cup / 100 g / 4 oz pecan nuts
1 cup / 100 g / 4 oz self-raising flour*
1 tsp bicarbonate of soda
½ cup / 75 g / 3 oz cocoa powder
⅓ cup / 50 g / 2 oz ground almonds
1 cup / 225 g / 8 oz soft dark brown sugar
1 cup / 225 g / 8 oz butter, diced
3 eggs, beaten
4 tbsp single (light) cream

*Where self-raising flour is not available use plain flour
and 1 extra tsp of baking powder.
Set the oven at 325 F / 160 C / Gas 3.

Grease and line 2 × 17.5 cm / 7 inch square cake tins
(pans).

Using the metal blade, process the nuts till coarsely
chopped. Set aside. Process the flour with the bicarbonate, cocoa powder, and ground almonds for 5
seconds, using the metal blade. Add the sugar and butter, and process for 4 to 5 seconds till just mixed. Add the
eggs and cream and process till smooth. Stop the
machine and stir in the nuts using a spatula. Spoon into
the tins and bake for 50 minutes till just firm to the touch.
Cool in the tins then cut into 10 squares.

CREAM BUNS

The hard part when making choux pastry is beating the eggs into the flour mixture. The processor makes light work of this.

Makes 12
Choux pastry:
4 tbsp / 50 g / 2 oz butter
⅝ cup / 150 ml / ¼ pint water
½ cup / 65 g / 2½ oz plain flour
pinch salt
½ tsp castor sugar
2 eggs, lightly beaten
Filling:
Cream and Hazelnut filling (page 106)
Topping:
1⅔ cups / 225 g / 8 oz icing sugar, sifted
1½ tsp strong coffee, freshly made

Set the oven at 400 F / 200 C / Gas 6.

Grease 2 to 3 baking sheets.

Put the butter and water into a medium-size pan. Heat gently to melt the butter, then rapidly bring to the boil. Remove from the heat, and quickly sift in the flour, salt and sugar. Beat with a wooden spoon to mix, then return to low heat and beat until the mixture forms a smooth, shiny ball.

Leave to cool, then tip into the processor fitted with the plastic blade. Process for a couple of seconds, then gradually pour in the eggs through the feed tube, with the machine running.

Process for a further 5 seconds or until the mixture is stiff and glossy.

Spoon into a piping bag fitted with a 1 cm / 1½ inch plain tube and pipe 12 buns on to the baking sheets. Bake in the heated oven for 30 minutes until crisp and golden.

Remove from the oven and make a small hole in the side of each bun to allow the steam to escape. Return to the oven for a further 5 minutes to dry out.

Cool on a wire rack, then split and fill with the cream and hazelnut mixture.

To make the topping. Put the icing sugar and coffee into a pan. Beat until smooth then heat gently, stirring well, for a minute, until the topping is glossy. Spoon over the buns and allow to set. Serve within 2 hours.

MUESLI SCONES

*These scones have a lovely nutty flavour,
and crunchy texture.*

Makes 10 to 12
1½ cups / 175 g / 6 oz wholemeal plain flour
½ cup / 50 g / 2 oz sugar-free muesli
4 heaped tsp baking powder
3 tbsp / 40 g / 1½ oz butter, diced
3 tbsp / 40 g / 1½ oz demerara sugar
1 egg
¾ cup / 175 ml / 6 fl oz single (light) cream

Set the oven at 425 F / 220 C / Gas 7.

Grease 2 baking sheets.

Put the flour, muesli, baking powder, butter and demerara sugar into the processor fitted with the metal blade. Process for 5 seconds till well-mixed. Beat the egg with the cream and pour into the processor through the feed tube with the machine running. Turn out on to a well-floured board and roll out to 2.5 cm / 1 inch thick. Cut into 3 cm / 1½ inch rounds with a plain biscuit cutter. Put shortbread on to the baking sheet and bake for 10 minutes till well-risen and golden. Serve warm.

A

apple and lemon pudding, steamed 104
apple and orange tart, quick 103
apple ice-cream, blackberry and 108
apple, Roquefort and walnut salad, beetroot 41
apples and onions, hot game pie with fried 58-9
apples stewed in wine 101
apricot dessert, frozen 112
apricots, fish risotto with 92
asparagus and egg Napoleon 27
avocado and blue cheese starter 23
avocado and ham, trout with 78

B

baby corn and green peppers, stir-fried beef with 55
bacon salad, warm potato and 44
beef with baby corn and green peppers, stir-fried 55
beetroot, apple, Roquefort and walnut salad 41
blackberry and apple ice-cream, 108
blue cheese pâté, quick 26
blue cheese starter, avocado and, 23
brownies 124
buns, cream 125

C

cabbage, crispy fried 37
cabbage leaves, stuffed 60
carrot soup from Germany 18
cashew nuts, Chinese chicken with pineapple and 56
cheesecake, rhubarb and ginger 111
cheese meatloaf, spiced lamb and 59
cheese pastry 22
cheese pâté, quick blue 26
cheese shortbreads 119
cheesy onion quiche 22
cheesy potato soup 12
cheesy ratatouille 35
chicken with pineapple and cashew nuts, Chinese 56
chicken stuffed with fruit and nuts 67
chicken soup, oriental 19
chilled summer soup, quick 17
Chinese chicken with pineapple and cashew nuts 56
chive cocottes, salmon and 79
chocolate crunch 121
chocolate macaroon pud 100
chocolate mousse cake 116
chop suey, vegetable 36
choux pastry 125
coconut curry, prawn (shrimp), pineapple and 93
cod provencale 76-7
coffee-time cake, Tina's 118
coffee walnut cake 122
cocottes, salmon and chive 79
coleslaw, curried 47
corned beef stuffed potatoes 54
country vegetable soup 15
courgette (zucchini) and fennel soup 13
cranberries, sauté of lamb with 58
cream buns 125
crispy fried cabbage 37
crumble, healthy rhubarb 99
crunch, chocolate 121
crunch, gingered pear 95
crunchy pastry 25
crunchy pepper and tuna mousse 28
curried coleslaw 47
curried lentil soup 16
curry-fried turkey 61
curry, prawn (shrimp), pineapple and coconut 93

D

date, lemon and walnut sponge pudding 97
dill sauce, Swedish meatballs with soured cream and 50
duck breasts with hazelnuts and orange potato balls 70

E

easy fruit cake 120
easy liver pâté 24
egg Napoleon, asparagus and 27

F

fennel and lemon sauce, lamb with 64
fennel salad 46
fennel soup, courgette (zucchini) and 13
fish and vegetable timbales 58-9
fish risotto with apricots 92
fish salad, smoked 91
five vegetable gratin 34
flapjacks, fruity 123
fresh tomato and vodka soup 14
fried apples and onions, hot game pie with 68-9
fried pork with mushrooms and water chestnuts 57
Frinton fruit tart 96
frozen apricot dessert 112
fruit and nuts, chicken stuffed with 67
fruit cake, easy 120
fruit pancakes 98
fruit tart, Frinton 96
fruity flapjack 123

G

game pie with fried apples and onions, hot 68-9
gâteau, hazelnut 106
gazpacho 21
ginger cheesecake, rhubarb and 111
gingered pear crunch 105
goujons with 'hot' tomato sauce 84
gratin, five vegetable 34
gratin, potato and anchovy (Jansson's Temptation) 32
green peppers, stir-fried beef with baby corn and 55

H

haddock with vegetables and cream 80
haddock mousse, hot 75
ham, trout with avocado and 78
hazelnut and orange potato balls, duck breasts with 70
hazelnut gâteau 106
hazelnut shorties 121
healthy rhubarb crumble 99
herby roulade 29
hot game pie with fried apples and onions 68-9
hot haddock mousse 75
'hot' tomato sauce, goujons with 84

I

ice-cream, blackberry and apple 108

J

Jansson's Temptation (potato and anchovy gratin) 32

K

kipper mousse quiche 25
kipper roulade 74

L

lamb and cheese meatloaf, spiced 59
lamb with cranberries, sauté of 58
lamb with fennel and lemon sauce 64
lemon and walnut sponge pudding, date, 97
lemon pudding, steamed apple and 104
lemon sauce, lamb with fennel and 64
lentil purée 41
lentil soup, curried 16
lime sorbet, mango and 102
lime tart 109
liver pâté, easy 24
liver stroganoff 52

M

macaroon pud, chocolate 100
mackerel with spiced walnut stuffing 82
mango and lime sorbet 102
mayonnaise 42
   avocado 42
   curry 42
   egg and chive 42
   garlic and herb 42
   green 42
   Marie-Rose 42
   soured cream 42
   tartare sauce 42
   watercress 42
   yogurt 42
meatballs with soured cream and dill sauce, Swedish 50
meatloaf, spiced lamb and cheese, 59
monkfish in whisky sauce with spinach timbales 86
mousse cake, chocolate 116
mousse, crunchy pepper and tuna 28
mousse, two trout 83

mousse, velvet 112
muesli scones 126
mushroom sauce 66
mushrooms and water
    chestnuts, fried pork with 57

N
nutty rice pilau 40
nuts, chicken stuffed with fruit
    and 67

O
onions, hot game pie with
    fried apples and 68-9
onion quiche, cheesy 22
orange potato balls, duck
    breasts with hazelnuts and 70
orange tart, quick apple and
    103
oriental chicken soup 19

P
pancakes, fruit 98
pâté, easy liver 24
pâté, quick blue cheese 26
pear crunch, gingered 105
pepper and tuna mousse,
    crunchy 28
pheasant Pojarski croûtes 65
pilau, nutty rice 40
pineapple and cashew nuts,
    Chinese chicken with 56
pineapple and coconut curry,
    prawn (shrimp), 93
pork Dijonnaise 62-3
pork with mushrooms and
    water chestnuts, fried 57
potato and bacon salad, warm
    44
potato balls, duck breasts with
    hazelnuts and orange 79
potato soup, cheesy 12
potato supper 38
potatoes, corned beef stuffed
    54
potatoes, spicy 33
prawn (shrimp), pineapple and
    coconut curry 93
provencal rice salad 45

Q
quiche, kipper mousse 25
quiche, cheesy onion 22
quick apple and orange tart
    103
quick blue cheese pâté 26
quick chilled summer soup 17
quick turkey à la king 71

R
rainbow salad 47
ratatouille, cheesy 35
rhubarb and ginger cheesecake
    111
rhubarb crumble, healthy 99
rice pilau, nutty 40
rice salad, provencal 45
risotto with apricots, fish 92
rissoles, seafood 85
ritzy pudding 110
rough puff pastry 27
roulade, herby 29
roulade, kipper 74

S
Salads:
    beetroot, apple, Roquefort
        and walnut 41
    fennel 46
    provencal rice 45
    rainbow 47
    seafood 90
    smoked fish 91
    tartare 42
    warm potato and bacon 44
salmon and chive cocottes 79
salmon and sole turban 81
sauces:
    hollandaise 81
    'hot' tomato 84
    mushroom 66
    tartare 42
sauté of lamb with cranberries
    58
scones, muesli 126
seafood rissoles 85
seafood salad 90
shortbreads, cheese 119
shorties, hazelnut 121
shrimp toasties 87
smoked fish salad 91
sole turban, salmon and 81
sorbet, mango and lime 102
soured cream and dill sauce,
    Swedish meatballs with 50
spiced lamb and cheese
    meatloaf 59
spiced walnut stuffing,
    mackerel with 82
spicy potatoes 33
spinach timbales, monkfish in
    whisky sauce with 86
sponge pudding, date, lemon
    and walnut 97
steamed apple and lemon
    pudding 104
stir-fried beef with baby corn

and green peppers 55
stuffed cabbage leaves 60
summer soup, quick chilled 24
Swedish meatballs with soured
    cream and dill sauce 50

T
tart, lime 109
tart, quick apple and orange
    103
timbales, fish and vegetable
    58-9
Tina's coffee-time cake 118
toasties, shrimp 87
tomato and vodka soup, fresh
    14
tomato sauce, goujons with
    'hot' 84
trout with avocado and ham
    78
tuna mousse, crunchy pepper
    and 28
turkey à la king, quick 71
turkey, curry-fried 61
two trout mousse 83

V
vegetable chop suey 36
vegetable gratin, five 34
vegetable soup, country 15
vegetables and cream,
    haddock with 80
vegetable timbales, fish and
    58-9
velvet mousse 112
vinaigrette 43
    chilli 43
    cream 43
    egg and herb 43
    garlic 43
    herbed 43
    Roquefort 43
vitello tonnato 51

W
walnut cake, coffee 122
walnut salad, beetroot, apple,
    Roquefort and 41
walnut sponge pudding, date,
    lemon and 97
walnut stuffing, mackerel with
    spiced 82
warm potato and bacon salad
    44
water chestnuts, fried pork
    with mushrooms and 57
whisky sauce with Spanish
    timbales, monkfish in 86

wine, apples stewed in 101

Z
zucchini *see* courgette